First World War
and Army of Occupation
War Diary
France, Belgium and Germany

20 DIVISION
Headquarters, Branches and Services
Commander Royal Engineers
21 July 1915 - 25 April 1919

WO95/2104/1

The Naval & Military Press Ltd
www.nmarchive.com
Published in association with The National Archives

Published by

The Naval & Military Press Ltd

Unit 10 Ridgewood Industrial Park,
Uckfield, East Sussex,
TN22 5QE England
Tel: +44 (0) 1825 749494

www.naval-military-press.com

www.nmarchive.com

This diary has been reprinted in facsimile from the original. Any imperfections are inevitably reproduced and the quality may fall short of modern type and cartographic standards.

© **Crown Copyright**
Images reproduced by permission of The National Archives, London, England, 2015.

Contents

Document type	Place/Title	Date From	Date To
Miscellaneous	2104/1 Comander Royal Engineers		
Heading	20th Division Divl Engineers C.R.E. Jly 1915-Apr 1919		
Heading	20th Division Headquarters 20th Division C.R.E. Vol I 21-31-7-15		
War Diary		21/07/1915	23/07/1915
War Diary	Lumbres	24/07/1915	26/07/1915
War Diary	Lynde	28/07/1915	28/07/1915
War Diary	Merris	29/07/1915	31/07/1915
Heading	CRE 20th Div. Vol. 9		
Heading	20th Division H.Q. 20th. Division C.R.E. Vol II August 15		
War Diary	Merris	02/08/1915	28/08/1915
Heading	20th Division H.Q. 20th Division C.R.E. Vol III Sept. 15		
War Diary	Noveau Monde	06/09/1915	30/09/1915
Heading	H.Q. 20th Division C.R.E. Vol 4 Oct. 15		
War Diary	Noveau Monde	01/10/1915	31/10/1915
Heading	H.Q. 20th. Division C.R.E. Vol. 5 121/7624 Nov 15		
War Diary	Nouveau Monde	01/11/1915	21/11/1915
War Diary	Sailly	22/11/1915	28/11/1915
Heading	CRE 20th Div. Vol. 6 121/7928 Dec 15		
War Diary	Sailly (Sheet 36 G. 22a)	02/12/1915	24/12/1915
War Diary	Sailly	25/12/1915	31/12/1915
Miscellaneous	C.R.E. Orders 8th December 1915	08/12/1915	08/12/1915
Heading	C.R.E. 20th Div. Vol. 7 January 1916		
War Diary	Sailly	01/01/1916	22/01/1916
War Diary	II Army area Oxelaere	22/01/1916	22/01/1916
War Diary	O.17a 6.4. (Sheet 27.)	28/01/1916	28/01/1916
Heading	C.R.E. XXth Div. Vol. 8		
War Diary	Ypres Salient A 23 Central Sheet 28	01/02/1916	28/02/1916
War Diary	Ypres Salient	01/03/1916	31/03/1916
War Diary	Sheet. 28. Ypres Salient	01/04/1916	16/04/1916
War Diary	Esquelbecque Sheet 27	17/04/1916	30/04/1916
War Diary	Esquelbecq (Sheet 27)	01/05/1916	18/05/1916
War Diary	Poperinge (Sheet 28)	19/05/1916	31/05/1916
War Diary	Poperinghe G.1. Sheet 28	01/06/1916	30/06/1916
Heading	20th Divisional Engineers C.R.E. 20th Division July 1916 Appendices Attached:- Report on Demolition of St. Jacques Church Ypres		
War Diary	Poperinge Sheet 28	01/07/1916	19/07/1916
War Diary	Bailleul Sheet 28	20/07/1916	23/07/1916
War Diary	Staple (Hazebrouck)	24/07/1916	25/07/1916
War Diary	Bus-Les-Artois (Leno II)	26/07/1916	29/07/1916
Diagram etc	Dugout Type A		
Diagram etc			
Miscellaneous	Report on the demolition of Ste Jacques Church Ypres.	30/06/1916	30/06/1916
Diagram etc	Secondary Charges of 7 Slabs Placed in Holes B.C.D.E.F.G & H		
Diagram etc			
Miscellaneous	20th Division Q/20/2820/5	11/07/1916	11/07/1916

Miscellaneous	20th Division Q/20/2820/1	06/05/1916	06/05/1916
Miscellaneous	Administrative Instructions in connection with relief of 20th Division by 6th Division.	11/07/1916	11/07/1916
Miscellaneous	20th Division 0/20/3842 Appendix A		
Miscellaneous	O.C. 83rd Company R.E.	12/07/1916	12/07/1916
Miscellaneous	OC. 83rd Field Coy R.E.	11/07/1916	11/07/1916
Miscellaneous	Reference enclosed Programme of Reliefs between 20th and 6th Div		
Miscellaneous	Relief of 20th Divisional Engineers by 6th Divisional Engineers.		
Map			
Heading	20th Divisional Engineers. C.R.E. 20th Division August 1916		
War Diary	Couin (LensII)	01/08/1916	16/08/1916
War Diary	Beauval (Sheet Albert)	17/08/1916	19/08/1916
War Diary	Treux (Sheet Albert)	20/08/1916	20/08/1916
War Diary	Forked Tree (L 26 b. 19 Sheet Albert)	22/08/1916	22/08/1916
War Diary	Advanced Divnl H qr (F 18. Sheet Albert)	23/08/1916	28/08/1916
Heading	C.R.E 20th Division September 1916 Appendices attached:- Report on Capture of Guillemont		
War Diary	Sheet Albert F 18 Minden Post	01/09/1916	03/09/1916
War Diary	Corbie	06/09/1916	10/09/1916
War Diary	Forked Tree Camp T 261.8	11/09/1916	17/09/1916
War Diary	Minden Post	18/09/1916	21/09/1916
War Diary	Treux	22/09/1916	27/09/1916
War Diary	Forkedtree	28/09/1916	29/09/1916
Miscellaneous	R.E. Report on the Capture of Guillemont Appendix A.	08/09/1916	08/09/1916
Map			
Map	Work done by 20th Divl		
Heading	20th Divisional Engineers C.R.E. 20th Division October 1916		
Heading	20 Division H.Q. C.R.E. Vol 16		
War Diary	Bernafay Wood S. 28.b.5.6 Sheet 57c S.W.	01/10/1916	15/10/1916
War Diary	Corbie A.8.a. (Albert Map 1/40000)	16/10/1916	24/10/1916
War Diary	Conde (S.W. Coruer of Lens Map 1/40000	25/10/1916	31/10/1916
Heading	20th Divisional Engineers. C.R.E. 20th Division November 1916		
War Diary	Conde S.W. Corner of Lens 11 Map 1/40000	01/11/1916	08/11/1916
War Diary	Picquigny	09/11/1916	14/11/1916
War Diary	Corbie	15/11/1916	30/11/1916
Heading	20th Divisional Engineers C.R.E. 20th Division December 1916		
War Diary	Corbie	01/12/1916	10/12/1916
War Diary	Briqueterie	11/12/1916	24/12/1916
War Diary	Corbie	25/12/1916	31/12/1916
Heading	War Diary of the H.Q.R.E. 20th Division January 1917 Vol 19		
War Diary	Corbie	01/01/1917	29/01/1917
War Diary	Heilly	01/02/1917	28/02/1917
War Diary	Heilly	01/02/1917	31/03/1917
Heading	20th Divisional Engineers War Diary For Month of April 1917 Vol 22		
War Diary	Somme Front	01/04/1917	28/04/1917
Heading	War Diary. of 20th Divisional Engineers. for month of May 1917 Vol 23		
War Diary	Havrincourt	01/05/1917	23/05/1917

War Diary	Queant Sector	21/05/1917	31/05/1917
Heading	War Diary of 20th Divl Engineers, for June 1917 Vol 27		
War Diary	Queant Sector	01/06/1917	30/06/1917
Heading	War Diary of 20th Divisional Engineers for July 1917		
War Diary		01/07/1917	31/07/1917
Operation(al) Order(s)	C.R.E.'s Operation Order No. 27	29/07/1917	29/07/1917
Heading	War Diary C.R.E HQ RS 20 D Vol 26		
War Diary		01/08/1917	31/08/1917
Operation(al) Order(s)	Operation Order No. 28 By C.R.E. 20th Division	04/08/1917	04/08/1917
Operation(al) Order(s)	C.R.E. 20th (Light) Division Operation Order No. 29	04/08/1917	04/08/1917
Miscellaneous	R.E. Material Notes.	04/08/1917	04/08/1917
Operation(al) Order(s)	Operation Order No. 30 by C.R.E., 20th Division	14/08/1917	14/08/1917
Heading	Diary C.R.E. 20th Divisional Engineers Sep. 1917 Vol 27		
War Diary	Proven Area	01/09/1917	10/09/1917
War Diary	Elverdinghe Pilckem and Lancemark	11/09/1917	30/09/1917
Operation(al) Order(s)	Operation Order No. 36 by C.R.E., 20th Division	17/09/1917	17/09/1917
Heading	HQ RS 20 D Vol 28		
War Diary	Proven	01/10/1917	02/10/1917
War Diary	Peromme	03/10/1917	09/10/1917
War Diary	Sorel-Le-Grand	10/10/1917	29/10/1917
Heading	HQ RS 20 D Vol 29		
War Diary	Sorel	01/11/1917	19/11/1917
War Diary	Heudecourt	20/11/1917	20/11/1917
War Diary	Villers Plouich	20/11/1917	30/11/1917
Heading	War Diary of 20th Division Engineers For December 1917 Vol 30		
War Diary	B Dugout Q 24C	01/12/1917	02/12/1917
War Diary	Sorel-Le-Grand	03/12/1917	03/12/1917
War Diary	Baizieux	04/12/1917	06/12/1917
War Diary	Hocqueliers	06/12/1917	11/12/1917
War Diary	Blaringhem	12/12/1917	14/12/1917
War Diary	Elzenwalle	14/12/1917	31/12/1917
Heading	War Diary of 20th Divisional Engineers January 1918 Vol 31		
War Diary	Elzenwalle	01/01/1918	06/01/1918
War Diary	Westoutre	07/01/1918	16/02/1918
War Diary	Blaringhem	17/02/1918	21/02/1918
War Diary	Ercheu (XVIII Corps Inf Amb)	22/02/1918	28/02/1918
Heading	20th Divisional Engineers C.R.E. 20th Division March 1918		
War Diary	Ercheu	01/03/1918	21/03/1918
War Diary	Ham	21/03/1918	22/03/1918
War Diary	Eppeville	22/03/1918	23/03/1918
War Diary	Nesle	23/03/1918	24/03/1918
War Diary	Rethonvillers	24/03/1918	24/03/1918
War Diary	Carrepuis	25/03/1918	25/03/1918
War Diary	Roye	25/03/1918	26/03/1918
War Diary	Le Quesnel	26/03/1918	28/03/1918
War Diary	Domart Sur-La-Luce	29/03/1918	30/03/1918
War Diary	Boves	30/03/1918	01/04/1918
War Diary	Namps-Au-Mont	02/04/1918	02/04/1918
War Diary	Quevauvillers	03/04/1918	08/04/1918
War Diary	Brocourt	09/04/1918	09/04/1918
War Diary	Huppy	10/04/1918	10/04/1918

War Diary	Gamaches	11/04/1918	17/04/1918
War Diary	Villers Chatel	18/04/1918	01/05/1918
War Diary	Villers-Au-Bois	02/05/1918	06/05/1918
War Diary	Chateau-De-La Haie	07/05/1918	30/06/1918
War Diary	Chateau-De-La-Haie N 12.C	01/07/1918	16/07/1918
War Diary	Chateau-De-La-Haie	17/07/1918	05/10/1918
War Diary	Villers Chatel	06/10/1918	30/10/1918
War Diary	Cambrai	31/10/1918	01/11/1918
War Diary	Auesmes-Lez-Auberi	03/11/1918	03/11/1918
War Diary	Vendigies	06/11/1918	07/11/1918
War Diary	Wargnies Le-Grand	08/11/1918	08/11/1918
War Diary	Bavai	09/11/1918	10/11/1918
War Diary	Feignies	11/11/1918	22/11/1918
War Diary	Nargnies Le-Grand	23/11/1918	25/11/1918
War Diary	Rieux	26/11/1918	30/11/1918
War Diary	Cambrai	01/12/1918	31/12/1918
War Diary	Pas	01/12/1918	25/04/1919
Heading	20th Division R.E. History of R.E.		
Heading	No. 3 Divl R E. H 9 & Units		
Miscellaneous	20th Divisional Engineers. Changes in Personnel.	10/03/1919	10/03/1919
Miscellaneous	Honours & Awards	15/03/1919	15/03/1919
Miscellaneous	N.C.O.'s & Men. Killed	15/03/1919	15/03/1919
Miscellaneous			
Miscellaneous	Lieut G.C. Marshall. RASC	12/03/1919	12/03/1919
Miscellaneous	Rolls on History of 84th Field & R.E.		
Miscellaneous	Wounded		
Miscellaneous	Killed, Missing and Died of Wounds.		
Miscellaneous	84 Field Corps During R.E.		
Miscellaneous	Notes For History of 96th Field Coy. R.E.		
Miscellaneous	Names of Commanding-Officers. Of 96 Field Coy. R.E.		
Miscellaneous	96th Field Company R.E.		
Miscellaneous	List of Officers. W.O's N C O.s Men Who Have Received Honours And Awards With 96th Field Coy RE		
Miscellaneous	Postal Section Offices		
Miscellaneous	An anxious time with the 20th Division Posts		

210411

Comande Reg. e Orgônicas

20TH DIVISION
DIVL ENGINEERS

C. R. E.
JLY 1915 - APR 1919

131/6250

Port Sudan

Headquarters 20th Division
C.R.E.
Vol: I

21-31-7-15

April '19

WAR DIARY – C.R.E. 20th Division –

INTELLIGENCE SUMMARY

Army Form C. 2118.

Place	Date	Hour	Summary of Events and Information	Remarks and references to Appendices
	July			
	21st.		Left Queensbury 1.15 p.m., arrived Southampton 3 p.m. & Embarked on S.S. "Courtfield" – Left Southampton 5.30 p.m.	
	22nd		Arrived Havre 5.45 a.m. & proceeded to No. 5 Rest Camp.	
	23rd		Entrained at Gare des Marchandises, & left at 12.19 p.m.	
LUMBRES	24th		Arrived LUMBRES 10 a.m. H.Q'rs No. 1 Sec'n 20th Sig. Co. had arrived, + SS Cable Section joined, on being attached to 20th Sig. Co.	
"	25th		84th Co. R.E. detrained at WIZERNES & went into billets at HALLINES.	HALLINES.
"	26th		96th " " " " " " " " " SETQUES	SETQUES.
"			83rd " " " " " " " " " LUMBRES	BOISDINGHEM.
LYNDE.	28th		Proceeded to LYNDE by march route.	
MERRIS.	29th		From LYNDE to MERRIS.	
"	30th		½ B'n. Durham L.I. to SWARTENBROUCK for water supply work.	
"			Field Co's reported their arrival in billets :- 83rd Co. OULTERSTEENE, 84th Co. LA BECQUE, 96th Co. NOOTE BOOM.	
"	31st.		One more Co. Durham L.I. to SWARTENBROUCK, for water supply work.	

S.M. Kenyon
Col. C.R.E., 20th Divn.

C.R.E. 20TH DIV:
VOL 9

131/6754

20th Division

H.Q. 20th Division C.R.E.

Vol. II

August 15

R.E. Head Qrs. 20th Division

WAR DIARY
or
INTELLIGENCE SUMMARY
(Erase heading not required.)

Army Form C. 2118

Place	Date	Hour	Summary of Events and Information	Remarks and references to Appendices
MERRIS	2nd		½-84th Co. proceeded to ERQUINGHEM for attached to 8th Div. for instruction.	
"	3rd		96th Co. proceeded to SAILLY for attached to 8th Div. for instruction.	
"	5th		Arranged for 3 wells to be sunk for supply in R.F.A. billeting area.	
"	7th		½-84th Co. proceeded to ERQUINGHEM, to join the other ½ Co. under instruction	
"	9th		Work commenced on 4-30yd. ranges under 83rd Co.	
"	10th		½-84th Co. returned to their former billet at LA BECQUE.	
"	17th		½-83rd Co. proceeded to BAC ST. MAUR, (to be attached to 8th Div. for instruction ½-84th Co. from ERQUINGHEM, ½-84th Co. from LA BECQUE, moved into billet near MERRIS formerly occupied by 83rd Co.	
"	19th		Adjutant + R.E. HdQrs. moved to SAILLY	
"	27th		84th Co. (less 2 sections) moved into billet vacated by 83rd Co. at N. MONDE. 83rd Co. (less 2 sections detached for Corps work) to LAVENTIE 96th Co. to LAVENTIE	
"	28th		R.E. Hd Qrs. moved from SAILLY to DISTILLERY, N. MONDE.	

S.R. Kenyon
Col. G.R.E. 20th Divn.

121/6997

20th Division

H.Q. 20th Div'n CRE.

vol III

Sept. 15.

Army Form C. 2118.

WAR DIARY
or
INTELLIGENCE SUMMARY.
(Erase heading not required.)

Instructions regarding War Diaries and Intelligence Summaries are contained in F.S. Regs. Part II. and the Staff Manual respectively. Title pages will be prepared in manuscript.

Place	Date	Hour	Summary of Events and Information	Remarks and references to Appendices
NOVEAU MONDE.	Sept. 6th	-	86th Cy move to billets at Rue de Brieile.	
"	7th		Lt. Plomer transferred to 2nd Cavalry Divn.	
"	8th		A. Co. D.L.I. arrived from Plinstrice. 101st Co. R.E. arrived for attachment for instruction.	
"	9th		2. Cpls. S. Stafford Regt (Res.) arrived for attachment & instruction. Lt. C.R. Anne joined for duty with 96th Cy.	
"	10th		1-section 96th Co. sent to ST-VENANT, to make smoke bombs.	
"	11th		Lt. Watson joined for duty with 96th Cy.	
"	12th		Civilian workmen demanded wages 4 fr. for May & 5 fr. Demand refused.	
"	13th		Lt. Morris left on duties as Adjutant. Capt. Reid left.	
"	16th		Civilian workmen returned to work on our terms.	
"	18th		Large Purchase of timber etc. to meet very heavy demands of Field Cys.	
"	21st		Re Operation Orders 10 & 11. Special instructions issued regarding use of Searchlights	
"	22nd		" " " " Special orders issued regarding working of Pontoon Bridges.	
"	24		Detachment of "D" D.L.I. ordered to rejoin their H.Q. on 26th inst. Searchlights used	
"			Advance stores established at Divisional front line. on Salient N.8 & 5.2.	

WAR DIARY
or
INTELLIGENCE SUMMARY.
(Erase heading not required.)

Army Form C. 2118.

Place	Date	Hour	Summary of Events and Information	Remarks and references to Appendices
NOV & NOV MONDE	25th		Safe wiring operations begun in 60th Bde front; unable to complete L."Haycraft" wounded.	
"	27th		Instructions from 2nd Lieut Enys regarding preparation of Communication trenches for drainage to time.	
"	28th			
"	29th		2nd Lt R.A. Baynter joined for duty with 83rd Coy.	
"	30th		Recommendations sent to 60th Inf. Bde regarding work required in area taken over from Mount Sorrel.	
"	31st		2nd Lt Rathbone later transf'd to Field Coys regarding the laying & shelters for wire also regarding charge of Defended Posts.	

Casualties during September.
Officers. wounded. 1.
Other Ranks. Killed 3. wounded 12. Died of wounds 3.
Died in Hospital (Pneumonia) 1.

J Minami
for CRE, XX Div RE.

[Stamp: COMMANDING ROYAL ENGINEERS, 20TH (LIGHT) DIVISION, 1 OCT 1915]

121/7593

H.Q. 20th Division CRE.

Vol 4

Oct 15

SECRET

WAR DIARY
or
~~INTELLIGENCE SUMMARY~~

Army Form C. 2118

Instructions regarding War Diaries and Intelligence Summaries are contained in F. S. Regs., Part II. and the Staff Manual respectively. Title pages will be prepared in manuscript.

(Erase heading not required.)

[Stamp: COMMANDING ROYAL ENGINEERS, 2 – NOV. 1915, 20th (LIGHT) DIVISION]

Place	Date	Hour	Summary of Events and Information	Remarks and references to Appendices
NIVEAU MONDE	1.10.15		96" Field Coy moved to billets in Lavente. Lt Lang & Section 96" Field Coy went to Scott Montain. ST-VENANT	
	2.10.15		Detailed instructions issued to Field Coys regarding number & construction of hut-shelters.	
	4.10.15		Meeting of O.C's Field Coys regarding drainage scheme.	
	7.10.15		Weekly Conference of C.R.E's established at office of C.R.E. 8" Div.	
	9.10.15		Lt Hugh-Jones wounded in torpedo mine-cutting expedition to enemy lines.	
	11.10.15		Lt Wade arrived to replace Lt Hugh-Jones.	
	13.10.15		Operation Order No 15, issued at. Lt Grant reported wounded.	
	14.10.15		Lt Grant 96" Field Coy died of wounds.	
	19.10.15		Ditches between front-line & Lavente cleared. chance for drainage.	
	21.10.15		14-15 data. Huts completed 41. Sandbags laid 7 miles.	
	22.10.15		Commenced work on entrenchments in staircase mining turfs; A facsimile of German line in front of our lines which is intended to attack.	
	25.10.15		Instructions issued to Field Coys re. operation order No 17.	
	27.10.15		L/Cpl. M. Broleomb, Hannan died of wounds.	
	28.10.15		Spr Johnson 96" Field Coy. awarded D.C.M.	
	29.10.15		Labourers issued 683" Jolly re: advancing line at Duck's Bill.	
	30.10.15		Entrenchments & report on demolition of Tuneries with Limestone.	
	31.10.15		Commenced repair of main road with slag.	

E.H.Kenyn
COL. C.R.E. 20TH DIVN.

No. 20 to Sec:
CCE.
Vol: 5
121/7634

Nov 15

Secret

Army Form C. 2118.

Instructions regarding War Diaries and Intelligence Summaries are contained in F. S. Regs., Part II. and the Staff Manual respectively. Title pages will be prepared in manuscript.

WAR DIARY
or
INTELLIGENCE SUMMARY.
(Erase heading not required.)

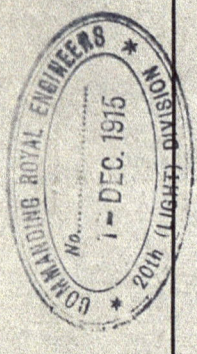

COMMANDING ROYAL ENGINEERS
1 - DEC. 1915
20th (LIGHT) DIVISION

Place	Date	Hour	Summary of Events and Information	Remarks and references to Appendices
Nouveau Monde	Nov. 1st/3rd		New Cia at Duck's Bill successfully carried out	
	4th		Lieut. E.B. Hugh Jones awarded Military Cross for services on wire cutting expedition when torpedoes were used.	
	5th		Lt. P. Bazeley reported for duty with 96th Field Coy. R.E. Lt./L. Train transferred from 84th to 2nd in command 96th Coy. Lt. R.H. Wards transferred from 96th to 84th Coy.	
	14th		83rd Fd Coy withdrawn from 60th Bde front line to rest.	
	15th		83rd commenced work on Light railway from Canal to Estaires-Sailly Road.	
	19th		D.L.I. commenced two corduroy tracks from Canal to Estaires-Sailly Main Road. Advance parties from 83rd & 84th Fd. R.E. take over from 6th Division R.E. Guards Div. R.E. administered parties around to take over.	
	20th		83rd & 84th A R.E. move to Bac St Maur. 83rd Coy R.E. take over from 2nd Hy R.E. front line from M.6.6.8.10 to W.10.6.9. 10-60 is Bde front. 84th Coy take over from 15th Coy from W.8.d.0.8. to W.6.6.8.10. 61st Bde new front.	
	21st		96th Fd Coy R.E. move to new billets at SAILLY vacated by 1st Home Countries R.E.(T) & come into Divl. Reserve in place of 83rd Coy.	

# WAR DIARY or INTELLIGENCE SUMMARY.

Army Form C. 2118.

Place	Date	Hour	Summary of Events and Information	Remarks and references to Appendices
SAILLY	Nov. 2nd		HdQrs R.E. 20th Div. moved to new billet at Sailly vacated by 1st Division	
	28th		Lt. J. W. Moore R.E. Adjt. went on leave to U.K. Lt. R.W. Dennis took over duties of Adjutant.	

Col. C.R.E., 20TH DIVN.

CRE. 20 7^e Div:
rot: 6

121/928

Dec 15

SECRET   Sheet I.

WAR DIARY
of
H.Qrs XX.th Divn R.E.
INTELLIGENCE SUMMARY.
Army Form C.2118.

(Erase heading not required.)

Instructions regarding War Diaries and Intelligence Summaries are contained in F. S. Regs., Part II. and the Staff Manual respectively. Title pages will be prepared in manuscript.

Place	Date	Hour	Summary of Events and Information	Remarks and references to Appendices
SAILLY. (Sheet 36 G.22 A)	2nd Dec.		Lt. NORMAN. 84th Field Cy R.E. wounded while supervising working party. A/ffc of CELLARS FARM Sheet 36 - N.10.C.	
	5th		In accordance with Divnl O.O. 27. the 96th Field Cy relieved the 84th Fd. Cy in the RIGHT SECTION & was affiliated for work in the front line to 59th Bde.	
	8th		Congratulations received from G.O.C. 11 Army & G.O.C. 3rd Corps on the complimentary report of the XI "Corps on taking over line of 20th Divn.	
	12th		Divnl O.O. No 30 received re preparation for fur attack, to be made, other names regarding fittings in of explosives in J in front parapet.	
	13th		Rept. of RIVER LYS at SAILLY BRIDGE. 15 ft 0½" (10ft nomaceny5ft) Causing heavy floods.	
	15th		In accordance with Divnl O.O. 29. 84th Fd Cy relieved the 253rd Fd Cy in the LEFT SECTION of the line & was affiliated to 61st Bde for work informent area	
	18th		2/Lt C.A.CURRIE reported wounded while supervising work in front line at WELL FARM SALIENT Sheet 36 - N.6.a.	
	19th		Lt. CURRIE died of wounds.	
	24th		Divnl O.O.31. Cancelled & O.O. 32 substituted. Notified that supply of timber at BASE temporarily nearly exhausted and hutting except huts were to be restricted.	

[Cont'd]

SECRET

Sheet 2.

WAR DIARY
or
INTELLIGENCE SUMMARY.
(Erase heading not required.)

Army Form C. 2118

Place	Date	Hour	Summary of Events and Information	Remarks and references to Appendices
SAILLY.	25th Dec.		In accordance with 20 Divnl O.O. No. 33. 96th Field Coy. relieved the forward area by 83rd Fd.Coy. and the latter Coy. affiliated to 60th Bde. for work in forward area.	
	25th "		Major H.S.CHRISTIE took over duties as acting C.R.E. during absence of Col. E.R.KENYON. Provisional orders issued regarding relief by 5th Divn.	
	31st "		Bgth of RIVER LYS at SAILLY BRIDGE 14ft-9½ ins. Causing heavy floods. The Ravensaré Rd. have been at work throughout the month in the same area (Sheet 36 from N.6.b.8.10 to N.5.a.0.5 near PETILLON) on the right flank GUARDS. Division, on the left flank 13th division. Heavy floods about the 13th & 25th inst. have greatly impressed all engineering work, an outstanding feature being the enormous quantity of water lying all over the country with only moderate rainfall. The natural drainage of the country being absolutely inadequate to take care of the large amount of water & prevent floods. There have been no other unusual occurences from an engineering point of view.	

M.S. Christie
Major
for Col, C.R.E. 20TH DIVN.

CRE's Orders 8th December 1915

The C.R.E. has great pleasure in publishing the following Special Order by G.O.C 20th Div. and thanks the Field Coys, Signal Coys and XI th D.L.I Pioneers and Divnl Cyclists for their share in the work.

Special Order

The G.O.C. 20th Division has much pleasure in publishing the following letter from G.O.C. XI th Corps and the remarks of the G.O.C 1st Army & 3rd Corps and in doing so adds:—
I wish to thank my staff commanders and all ranks of the Division for their good and strenuous work which has produced this gratifying result.

Sgd R. H. Davies Major Genl
Commanding 20th Divn

XI th Corps
G. 360

Adv 1st Army

I wish to bring to the notice of the Army Commanders the state of the defences taken over by me from 20th Divn. They were far better and it is evident that far more work has been put into them than in any part of the new line I have taken over and if considered right I should like my thanks together with the thanks of the thanks of the G.O.C. Guards Division conveyed to the G.O.C 20th Division.

XI th Corps. Hd Qrs
28th Nov. 1915

Sgd R. Haking
Lt General
Commanding XI th Corps

CREs Orders Continued

Please convey to Major General R.H. Davies Commanding and all ranks of the 20th Division my hearty congratulations on the results of their work.

5. Dec. 1915.

Sgd D. Haig Genl
Commanding First Army

20th Division

The Corp Commander is very glad to be able to forward these remarks by the First Army Commander and desires to add his congratulations

Sgd C.F. Romer,
Brig Genl
General Staff

C.R.E. Lot's Div"

Vol. 7
January 1916

SECRET

Hd Qrs R.E.
26 Division [↑ 4 Division]

Army Form C. 2118.

WAR DIARY
or
INTELLIGENCE SUMMARY

(Erase heading not required.)

[Stamp: COMMANDING ROYAL ENGINEERS 2 FEB 1916 20th (LIGHT) DIVISION]

Place	Date	Hour	Summary of Events and Information	Remarks and references to Appendices
SAILLY	1916. 1st Jan		Divisional front from near BREWERY N.6.d.8-10. & PETILLON N.8 & 8. (Sheet 36). on the right flank. GUARDS Division on the left. 13th Division on the left.	
	5th		Lieut R.N.JERVIS 83rd Field Coy. killed while superintending looking Parties near EATON HALL N 3 (Sheet 36).	
	9th		84th Field Coy. moved to billets at DISTILLERY NOYEAUMONDE (Sheet 36) and other to work on RESERVE LINE under orders of 3rd Corps.	
	10th		96th Field Coy. left forward area for Corps Reserve area, filling VIEUX BERQUIN AREA (Sheet 36A)	
	11th		83rd Field Coy. left forward area for Corps Reserve area, filling VIEUX BERQUIN AREA (Sheet 36A)	
	12th		R.E. Hd Qrs. left forward area for Corps Reserve area. New Hd Qrs. MORBECQUE D.25.c.3.4 (Sheet 36A).	
	11th		"A" Field Coy. minus Corps Reserve area. Hd Qrs. MORBECQUE D.25.c.S.1. (Sheet 36A)	
	12th		85th Field Coy. minus Corps Reserve area. Hd Qrs. MORBECQUE D.25.c.1.2. (Sheet 36A)	
	13th		Enemy comment.	
	16th		Lieut P.E. NORMAN formerly reported wounded returned to duty. Hall 96 Fld Coy.	
	21st		83rd & 96th Field Coys. in relief to the Corps Commander. 85th Fld Coy. moved from 2nd Division area to the Reserve from Billetts (HAZEBROUCK SA) ½ mile S. of MORBECQUE CHURCH.	
	22nd		Divisional R.E. moves from 1st Army to 2nd Army.	

SECRET SHEET 2   H.Q. R.E.
                      20th Division

WAR DIARY
or
INTELLIGENCE SUMMARY.
(Erase heading not required.)

Army Form C. 2118.

Place	Date	Hour	Summary of Events and Information	Remarks
Army Area	1916			
ONELAERE	22nd Jan		H.Q. 2nd R.E. O.17.a.6.4. — 83rd Fd. Coy. H.18.d.4.4. P.24 & 25 (Sheet 27). — 82nd Field Coy	
O.17.a.6.4. (Sheet 27)			killed H.11.c.8.4. — 96th Field Coy. G.6.b.1.1. J.26 & J.29. — 4th Army 20th Signal Coy	
	28th		with Divisional H.Qrs. O.17.b.2.3. (Sheet 27).	
			Two sections of 96th Field Coy forward to forward area attached to	
			14th Division H.7.c.77. (Sheet 28) for hutting etc.	

E.P. Kenyon
COL. C.R.E. 20TH DIVN.

C. R. E.
XXth Div.

Vol. 8

SECRET

WAR DIARY Hd Qrs. R.E.
or
INTELLIGENCE SUMMARY. XX Div.

Army Form C. 2118.

Place	Date	Hour	Summary of Events and Information	Remarks and references to Appendices
YPRES. SALIENT. A23 Central Sheet 28.	February 1st		Division in "Rest". H'dQrs. R.E. Oxelaere. 83 "Fd Cy R.E. at St SYLVESTRE. 84 "Fd Cy R.E. ARNEKE. 96 "Fd Cy. LE BUNDER (all Sheet 27).	
	3rd		H'dQrs R.E. moved from OXELAERE to ESQUELBECQUE. 84 "Fd Cy R.E. from ARNEKE to LEDRINGHEM (Sheet 27).	
	4th		96 "Field Cy. from LE BUNDER to HERZEELE (Sheet 27)	
	5th		83 "Field Cy. from ST SYLVESTRE to WATOU (Sheet 27).	
	11th		83 "Fd Cy move from WATOU to new billets in forward area A23c (Sheet 28). Half Coy in CANAL BANK affiliated to 60" Inf Bde. Eqpt Bee front from F34 to E26 being left flank of Army. On Divison left flank 59 "Inf Regt. 96" Fd Cy R.E. from HERZEELE to new billets in forward area A23a Sheet 28. Half Cy in CANAL BANK affiliates to 59 "Inf Bde holding Regt Bde front from E23 to B16. On Divison right flank 6 "Division.	
	12th		82 Field Cy move from LEDRINGHEM to WATOU (sheet 27). H'dQrs R.E. move from ESQUELBECQUE to WATOU (sheet 27) 84 "Field Cy R.E. move from WATOU to forward area A23 central (sheet 28) & 96 "(sheet 28). Half Coy in CANAL BANK both now maintenance of Comm Bridges from	
	13th		Coy in CANAL BANK both now maintenance of Comm Bridges from 83rd + 96 "Field Coys.	

Sheet II
SECRET

WAR DIARY
or
INTELLIGENCE SUMMARY.

H⁰ Qu RE VIII Divn.

Army Form C. 2118.

(Erase heading not required.)

Instructions regarding War Diaries and Intelligence Summaries are contained in F. S. Regs., Part II. and the Staff Manual respectively. Title pages will be prepared in manuscript.

Place	Date	Hour	Summary of Events and Information	Remarks and references to Appendices
YPRES SALIENT A 23 c 5 & 6.1 Sheet 28.	16ᵗʰ		Col. Kenyon. left 26ᵗʰ Divn to take up duties as C.E. 4ᵗʰ Corps.	
	17ᵗʰ		Lᵗ Col. A. Rolland. Took over duties of CRE XX Divn.	
	27/28 night		84ᵗʰ Field Coy relieved 83ʳᵈ Field Coy in Left Sector + now affiliated to 6ᵗʰ Inf. Bde.	

A. Rolland
Lᵗ Col. G.R.E. 20ᵗʰ Divn.

SECRET

HdQrs 20 "Divn R.E.
A 23 central sheet 25.
Army Form C. 2118.

WAR DIARY
or
INTELLIGENCE SUMMARY.
(Erase heading not required.)

Place	Date	Hour	Summary of Events and Information	Remarks and references to Appendices
YPRES SALIENT.	March 1st		Divisin left flank of British Army. Divisnl front stopt flank from junction with Canal Divisin on Canal Bank at B.13.d.9.7. Sheet 28 to C.14.d.5.7 Sheet 28 joining 6 Divn. 82nd Field Coy R.E. detailed for work in 59th Brigade front- Right. 96 " " " " " " " " 83 " " " in reserve: maintaining Canal Bridges and working on Railways & Tunnels. Most of Canal Bank.	[STAMP: COMMANDING ROYAL ENGINEERS 10 APR. 1916 20th (LIGHT) DIVISION]
	26th		Capt P.E. Middleton O.C. 84 Field Cy R.E. killed while inspecting funnel in No man's land in front of BARNSLEY ROAD C.7.c.10.4. Sheet 28.	
	31st		Work on wiring, reclaiming trenches & jumping of Butts proceeded throughout the month but was greatly impeded by rain and snow. The disposition of Works R.E. and Field Cys R.E. remained the same during the month.	

A. Bevan
Lieut. Col. R.E.
C.R.E. 20th Divn

SECRET

Army Form C. 2118.

Vol 10

WAR DIARY
or
INTELLIGENCE SUMMARY.

(Erase heading not required.)

H.Q. R.E. 20th Divn

Place	Date	Hour	Summary of Events and Information	Remarks and references to Appendices
SHEET 28. YPRES SALIENT.	April 1st		Routine of Front R.E. unchanged since last report. Reconnoitring on left flank of Divisional Sector & billetting & billetting Area from June 1st with Junct. Divn on the left at CANAL BANK at B12.a.7.J to June 14th with Guards Divn on the right at C11.d.57. 84th & 96th Field Coys remain affiliated to Left and Right Brigades respectively working on organisation & general supervision of wire work, revetment of trenches, reinforcing trenches destroyed by enemy shell fire, and constructing new emplacements & machine gun emplacements. 83rd Field Coy employees mainly occupied in making Canal Bridges and constructing new ones, also maintaining & keeping up tramways over Canal Bank.	
	15th		Commencement of R.E. relief by 6th Divn.	
	16th		84th Field Coy entrained at POPERINGHE for CALAIS for a course of training.	
ESQUELBECQUE Sheet 27.	17th		96th " " March to HERZEELE for training also took charge of 85th work in Large Reserve Camp.	
	18th		83rd March to WINNEZEELE for training also supervise training of 28 K.R.R. Pioneers.	

SECRET   Sheet 2.

Army Form C. 2118.

WAR DIARY
or
INTELLIGENCE SUMMARY.
(Erase heading not required.)

H.Qrs. R.E.
26th Divn.

Place	Date	Hour	Summary of Events and Information	Remarks and references to Appendices
	26"		2nd F. Coy. moved from CALAIS on route for HERZEELE. 93rd F. Coy. entrained for CALAIS.	
	27" 28"		96 F. Coy. moved to billets at WINNEZEELE. During the period in reserve training has been carried out according to prepared programmes. Details to drill & mastering of R.E. training, bridging, demolitions & defence of villages etc. have been carried out. Lectures & tactical instruction has been given to infantry in trench warfare. During afternoons & evenings sports & concerts have been encouraged.	Maythorpe Major R.E. a/CRE 26 Divn.

Maythorpe
Major R.E.
a/CRE 26 Divn.

SECRET.

WAR DIARY Hd. Qrs. R.E. 20th Division.

INTELLIGENCE SUMMARY

(Erase heading not required.)

Army Form C. 2118.

Vol II

Stamped: COMMANDING ROYAL ENGINEERS 6 JUN 1916 20th (LIGHT) DIVISION

Signed: Lt-Col. C.R.E. 20th Div.

Place	Date	Hour	Summary of Events and Information	Remarks and references to Appendices
ESQUELBECQ. (Sheet 27)	MAY. 1.		Divisional R.E. in Reserve Area for training etc. Headquarters R.E. ESQUELBECQ. C.7.b.9.1. Sheet 27. 83rd Fd. Co: R.E. CALAIS. Large Rest Camp. 84th ,, ,, ,, HERZEELE D.10.c.2.7. } Sheet 27. 96th ,, ,, ,, WINNIZEELE, J.17.a.8.6. }	
	2.		Two sections of 84th Co: detailed to relieve 96th Co: in CANAL BANK north of YPRES to work under the C.E. XIVth Corps on remaking of L defences.	
	6.		83rd Field Co: leave CALAIS and march to ZUTKERQUE en route for LEDRINGHEM.	
	7.		,, ,, ,, march to BOLLEZEELE en route for LEDRINGHEM.	
	8.		,, ,, ,, arrive LEDRINGHEM.	
	9.		Four sections of 96th Field Co: detailed for work on CANAL BANK and attached to Guards Division.	
	17.		83rd Field Co: march from LEDRINGHEM to WINNIZEELE.	
	18.		Commencement of relief of Guards Division by 20th Division. Headquarters R.E. from ESQUELBECQ to POPERINGHE.	
POPERINGE (Sheet 28)	19.		Four sections of 96th Field Co: rejoin unit from work in CANAL BANK. 84th Field Co: march from HERZEELE to A.28.d.6.2.) 83rd ,, ,, ,, ,, ,, WINNIZEELE to A.30.d.3.0.) Sheet 28. 96th ,, ,, ,, ,, ,, ,, ,, H.7.a.5.9.)	
	20.		84th Field Co: relieve 75th Field Co: Guards Division and were affiliated to 61st Infantry Bde. for work in front line area. 83rd Field Co: relieve 76th Field Co: Guards Division and were affiliated to 60th Infantry Bde. for work in front line area. 96th Field Co: took over work in back area. Divisional front from C.28.a.4.9. near WIELTJE to I.12.c.8.2. near MENIN road Sheet 28. Canadian Corps on Right Flank, 6th Division on Left Flank.	
	26.		59th Infantry Bde relieved 61st Infantry Bde., and 84th Field Co: were affiliated to 59th Inf:Bde: for work.	
	31.		Training programme when in reserve area was greatly upset by all Companies having to send up large parties to carry on work in forward area. On return to forward area Field Companies affiliated to Brigades were employed on general supervision and organization of Infantry labour employed in reclaiming and draining, also constructing new trenches and slits. 96th Field Co: were employed on exploring for cellars in YPRES, clearing and strengthening them for protection against shell fire; also general sapper work in back billet area.	

1577 Wt.W10791/1773 500,000 1/15 D.D.&L. A.D.S.S./Forms/C. 2118.

S E C R E T.

WAR DIARY
or
INTELLIGENCE SUMMARY.
(Erase heading not required.)

Army Form C. 2118.

Headquarters R.E.
20th Division.
========================

J U N E. 1 9 1 6.

Vol 12

Instructions regarding War Diaries and Intelligence Summaries are contained in F.S. Regs., Part II. and the Staff Manual respectively. Title pages will be prepared in manuscript.

Place	Date 1916.	Hour	Summary of Events and Information	Remarks and references to Appendices
POPERINGHE. G.I. Sheet 28.	JUNE. 1st.		Divisional area remained unchanged, extending from C.28.a.4.9. near MENIN ROAD (Sheet 28). Canadian Corps on Right Flank. 84th Field Company R.E. affiliated for work to 59th Brigade in Left Sector, 83rd Field Company R.E. affiliated to 60th Brigade for work in Right Sector. 96th Field Company R.E. in Reserve under C.R.E. working on support line &c.g and general R.E. work in back billet area.	
	6th.		Relief of 60th Bde. by 61st Bde. cancelled owing to great activity of enemy.	
	9th.		On completion of relief of 60th Bde. by 61st Bde. 83rd Co: were affiliated to 61st Bde. for work.	
	15th.		Divisional Headquarters and Headquarters R.E. transferred to new camp in Camp "C", A.30.	
	17th.		Divisional Headquarters and Headquarters R.E. ordered to return to billets at POPERINGHE.	
			On relief of 61st Bde by 60th Bde. 83rd Co: were affiliated to 61st Bde for work.	
	25th.		An R.E. reconnaissance party consisting of Lieut. H.S. MANISTY, one N.C.O. and three sappers, accompanied 59th Bde. raiding party on German trenches, C.29.central, in front of YPRES. R.E. party blew up two dugouts, one Observation Post and brought in four prisoners and other equipment. Lieut. MANISTY wounded and one sapper killed.	
	27th.		On relief of 59th Bde. by 61st Bde. 84th Co: became affiliated to 61st Bde for work.	
	29th.		An R.E. reconnaissance party, consisting of 2/Lieut. H.Y.V. JACKSON, one N.C.O. and five sappers, accompanied 60th Bde. raiding party on German trenches opposite H.16. and H.20., East of YPRES. Time was insufficient for a thorough search for mines. One prisoner was brought back. R.E. party suffered no casualties.	
	30th.		Throughout the month difficulty has been experienced in obtaining adequate transport for R.E. materials for front line and back billet areas. In addition to all available R.E. and Brigade transport, the following has been fully in use when obtainable:- 30 G.S. wagons supplied by Divisional R.A., 6 Pontoon wagons from section of Pontoon Park attached and Motor Lorries varying from 2 to 8 as available. Normally sufficient transport can be procured, but when operations are pending all lorries, and the majority of R.A. wagons, are suddenly withdrawn leaving a large shortage of transport for R.E. material.	

Lieut. Colonel R.E.
Commanding Royal Engineer, 20th Division.

20th Divisional Engineers.

C. R. E.

20th DIVISION

J U L Y 1 9 1 6

Appendices attached;-

Report on Demolition of St. Jacques Church YPRES

SECRET

WAR DIARY
or
INTELLIGENCE SUMMARY.

Army Form C. 2118.

H.Qrs. R.E. 26th Divn.
July Vol 13

Place	Date	Hour	Summary of Events and Information	Remarks and references to Appendices
APERINGHE Sheet 28	July 1916 1st		General are same as in last report, moving from C.28a near WIELTJE GTIC near MENIN R⁴ Canadian Divn on right flank. Guard Divn on left. 83ʳᵈ Field Cy working in Right Sector. 74ᵗʰ Field Cy in Left Sector. 96ᵗʰ Field Cy in reserve working in support lines & general work in back area.	
	5ᵗʰ		96ᵗʰ Field Cy relieved 74ᵗʰ Field Cy in forward area & sent officers & 6.37"/Bn Bde for work. 84ᵗʰ Jᵈ Cy become Cy in reserve.	
	15ᵗʰ		83ʳᵈ Fᵈ Cy ordered to be attached 65ᵗʰ Cofs & leave for 5ᵗʰ Corps area	
	16ᵗʰ		R.E. HQrs. relieved in line by 6ᵗʰ Divn R.E. and move to ESQUELBECQ (Sheet 27) Reserve area. 96ᵗʰ Fᵈ Cy, 74ᵗʰ & 2nd Lowland working in Z Defences, on relief by Fᵈ Cys of 6ᵗʰ Divn move to WINNEZEELE (Sheet 27) Cops Reserve area	
	17ᵗʰ		83ʳᵈ Fᵈ Cy on relief by Fᵈ Cy of 6ᵗʰ Divn move to HOOTKERQUE (Sheet 27) Cops Reserve area.	
	18ᵗʰ		Two sections of 96 Fᵈ Cy regmr. their work from Z Defences.	
	19ᵗʰ		On orders to move to 5ᵗʰ Corps area. 83ʳᵈ Fᵈ Cy move to billets near BERTHEN (Sheet 27)	
	20ᵗʰ		96ᵗʰ Fᵈ Cy. move to billet at LEDON (Sheet 36). R.E. Hqrs move to BAILLEUL (Sheet 28) are both over write from 26ᵗʰ Divn R.E.	
BAILLEUL Sheet 28	21ˢᵗ		83ʳᵈ Fᵈ Cy move to billets at DRANOUTRE (Sheet 28)	

WAR DIARY
or
INTELLIGENCE SUMMARY.

(Erase heading not required.)

Army Form C. 2118.

Place	Date	Hour	Summary of Events and Information	Remarks and references to Appendices
BAILLEUL (Sheet 27E)	22nd		86th Fd Coy report 2nd Div from 5th Corps. 53rd Fd Cy on relief by Fd Cy of 50th Divn moved to billets near ST JANS CAPPEL Sheet 36A	
	23rd		86th Fd Cy move to HONDEGHEM (Sheet 27). 96th Fd Cy after relief by Fd Cy of 50th Divn moved to billets at M12A Sheet 28	
STAPLE (HAZEBROUCK 5D)	24th		86th Fd Cy marched to entrain at CASSEL for DOULLENS — billetting party that night at HALLOY Sheet 5D R.E. HdQrs handed over work to CRE 36 (ULSTER) Divn and left for billets at STAPLE (HAZEBROUCK 5A) 83rd Fd Cy moved to billets at HONDEGHEM (Sheet 27)	
	25th		R.E. HdQrs move to entrain at CASSEL and depart for DOULLENS 1.30 p.m. 96th Fd Cy marched to entrain at HOPOUTRE for FREVENT and billeted at BOCQUE-MAISON (5D son) 83rd Fd Cy move to entrain at CASSEL for DOULLENS	
BUS-LES-ARTOIS (Sheet 11)	26th		R.E. HdQrs move to BUS-LES-ARTOIS. — 86th Fd Cy move to BUS-LES-ARTOIS. 96th Fd Cy move to AUTHIE (Sheet 11) — 83rd Fd Cy move to SARTON (Sheet 11)	
	27th		83rd Fd Cy move to VAUCHELLES (Sheet 11) — 96th Fd Cy move to ROSSIGNOL FARM (5D Sheet 11) + took over work from 38th Md Divn	
	28th		86th Fd Cy move to COURCELLES (Sheet 11) + took over work from Fd Cy of 38th Divn. 53rd Fd Cy move to HEBUTERNE (J.17.C.S.4. Sheet 57A) + took over work from Fd Cy 38th Divn	
	29th		Hd Qrs R.E. move to COUIN Chau (Sheet 11) + took over work from 38th Divn R.E. Divl front from K.17A to — UL 5 & Z H7d	

P.R. Ranaud Lt Col RE CRE II Divn
31/7/16

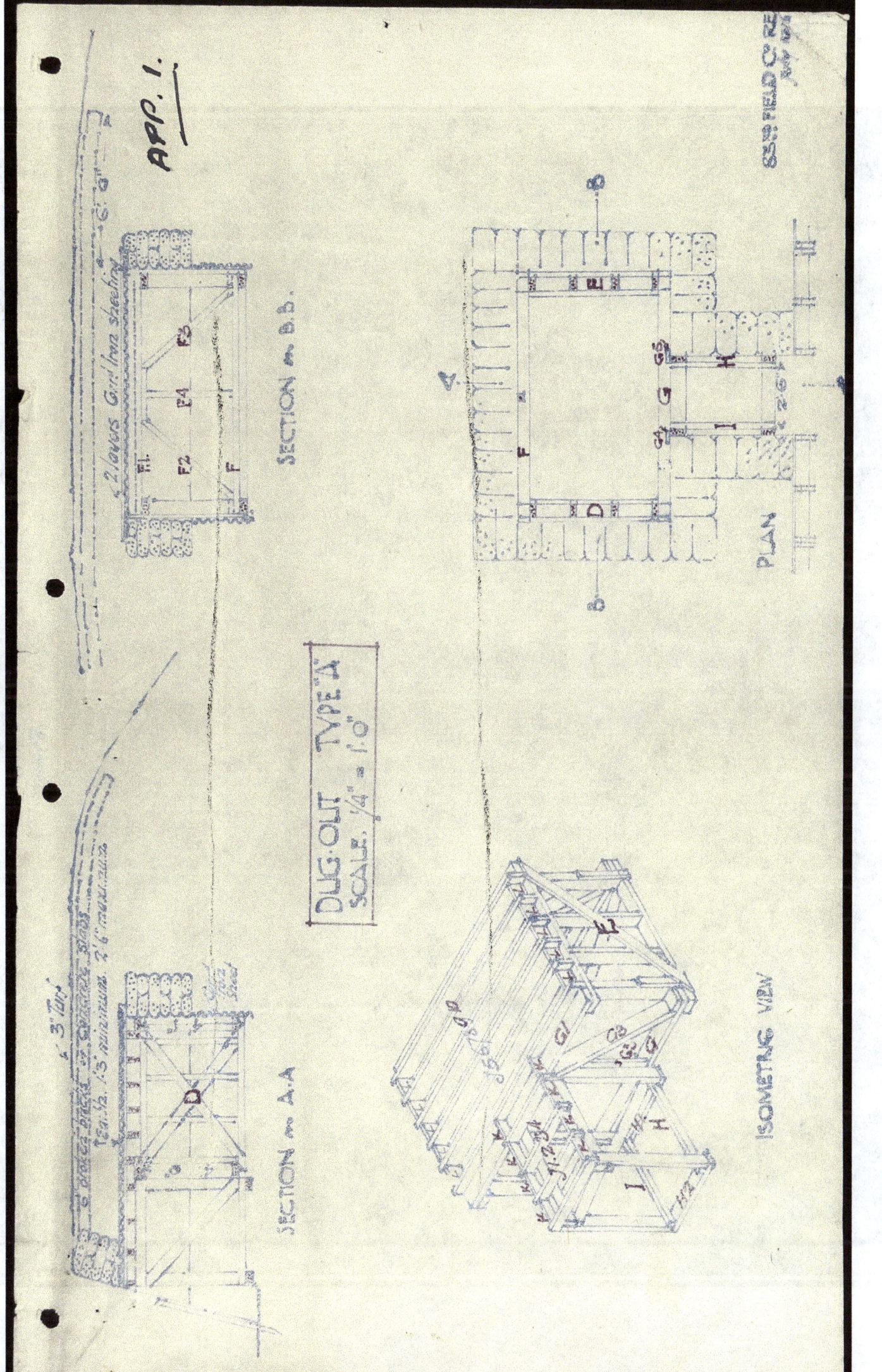

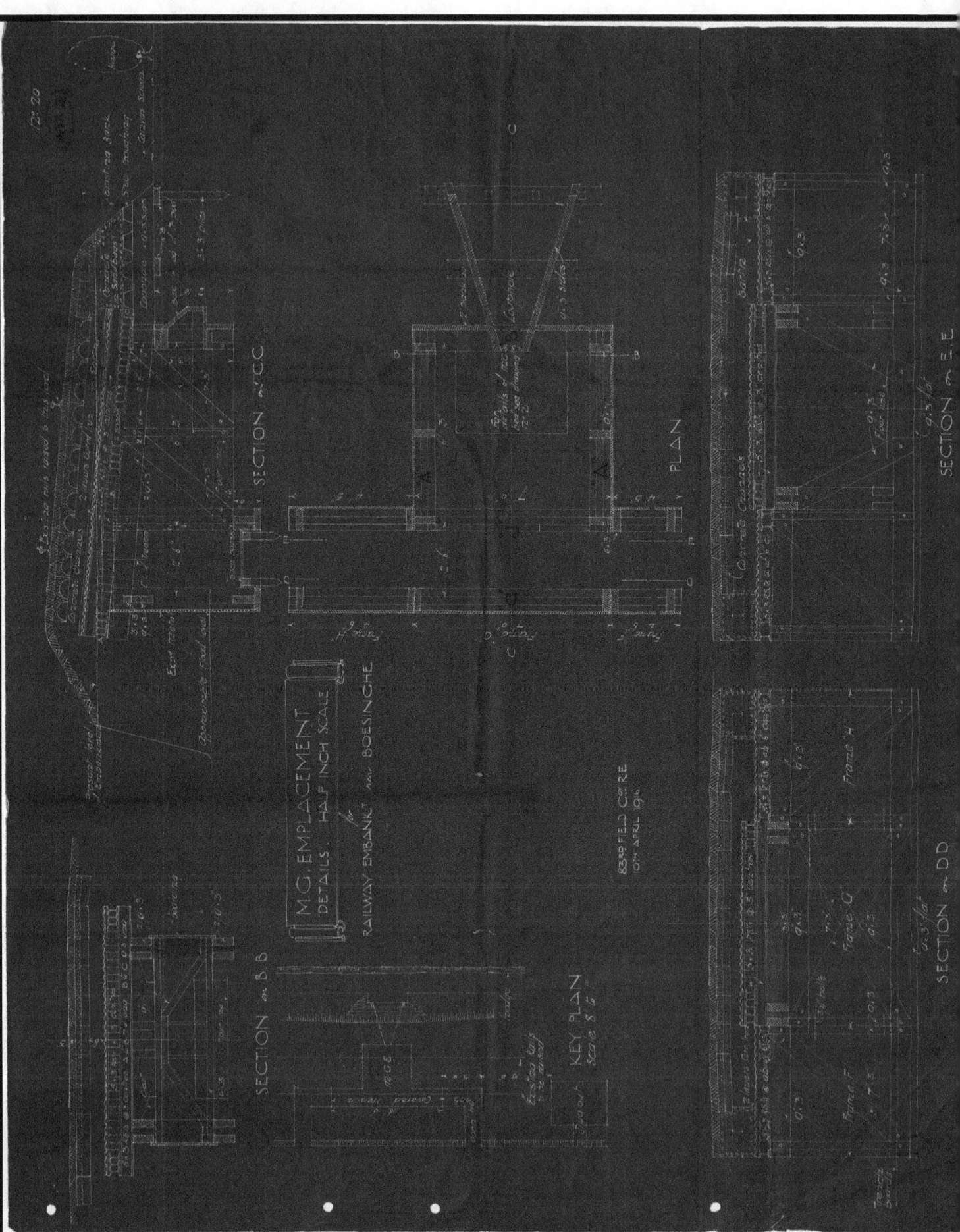

APP 3

Report on the demolition of ST^e JACQUES church YPRES
30th June 1916.

omit border of censor.

The church is situated near the Ramparts in YPRES, between the North and Central Sally Ports. It was thought that the tower was used by the Enemy as an observing point, and it was therefore decided to demolish it.

The remains of the tower at this time, 27th June consisted almost entirely of the west face a portion of which still attained its original height of 145 feet and which projected by itself for a height of 75 feet above either of the adjacent walls. The general appearance of the tower is shown in the sketch and it will be seen that practically all the weight was taken by the N.W. angle.

It was decided to demolish the tower by means of small charges in bore holes round the bases of the two ~~buttress~~ buttresses so as to avoid the danger of fragments long distances over the town as would have happened if one large charge had been employed.

A test hole 1½ inches diameter was bored in the wall at A (in the plan) to a depth of 3'4" and a charge of 20 1B primers, tamped with 14 inches of clay and broken brick, was exploded.

The result was curious. The original hole was merely enlarged to about 7 inches all through, and a few stones only were blown out.

It appeared that the brickwork inside the stone facing was so soft that nearly all the gas generated by the explosion was forced into the body of the wall opening

opening a large number of fissures but a crater in the outside facing of only about 1 foot diameter.

The result suggested the idea of blowing a series of similar charges round the buttresses, and if, as seemed probable, the tower remained standing and was merely shaken, of placing bigger charges in the enlarged holes.

This method was found to work excellently.

The accompanying plan shows the arrangement of the boreholes and the secondary charges. 20 1oz guncotton primers were placed in the boreholes, in their own tin tubes, and tamped with 14 inches of clay and broken-brick.

7 slabs of guncotton were afterwards placed in the holes B C D E F G H and well tamped with bricks and sandy clay. Both charges were fired electrically.

66 lbs of guncotton was the total amount of explosive used.

The result was that the tower fell in one piece towards the North West, having cracked off along the lines shown in the sketch.

This method of laying charges for the demolition of towers etc should work well in similar cases where the interior brickwork is of poor quality compared with the outside facing.

3/7/16

Ralph Bagnold
Lt R.E.
83rd Field Coy.

14 inches of clay & broken brick was used in each borehole as tamping.

N —|——|— S

1½ borehole

Detail showing result of 20 1 oz primers.

28'
4'
A
B
7'3"
C
5'3" D
E
F H
7'3" 6'9"
G
5'3"
25'

WEST FACE.

Secondary charges of 7 slabs placed in Holes B.C.D.E.F.G & H.

20th Division.
Q/20/2820/5.

....

Reference this Office Q/20/2820 of the 6th May 1916, regarding the handing over and taking over of trench and billet stores. The units enumerated in para: 2 B. of the above quoted letter will on relief by the 6th Division forward to Divisional Headquarters lists of trench and billet stores

      (a) Handed over to 6th Division.
      (b) Taken over from 6th Division
          in reserve area.

These lists should reach Divisional Headquarters as soon as possible after the relief is complete. Great care should be taken to ensure that all stores handed over both in the trenches and transport lines, are included in the lists.

Battalions passing through the "A", "B" and "C" Camps or POPERINGHE (provided they only stop one night) need not send in list of stores taken and handed over within the Division, except in the case of the last Battalion of this Division, which hands over to the 6th Division, which Battalion will forward complete list of stores handed over.

R.A.M. Bassett. Capt for
Lieut.Colonel,
A.A. & Q.M.G., 20th Division.

11/7/16.

Copies to:-
59th Brigade
60th Brigade
61st Brigade
11th. D.L.I.
C. R. A.
C. R. E.
Divn. Train.
A.D.M.S.
A.D.V.S.
D.A.D.O.S.
O. 1/c Baths & Laundry.

O.C.
Company R.E.

For necessary action in due course. Lists to be sent through this office. A Copy of the letter referred to above was sent to you under this office No.W/1645. A further copy is now attached.

12/7/16.

Captain R.E.
Adjutant R.E. 20th Division.

20th Division
Q/20/2820/1

The Transfer of Trench, Camp, and Billet stores from one division to another on relief:- or, within the division, from one brigade or unit to another on relief or change of billets, has hitherto been carried out in a manner, which from the point of view of results, leaves much to be desired.

(a). The system by which a list in duplicate of stores is made out by the outgoing unit and signed by an Officer of both the out and incoming unit, is quite simple.

(b). The rendering of incorrect returns to divisional headquarters is unnecessary and can only be the result of carelessness. Brigades and units must hold receipts for whatever stores they take or hand over - these receipts may be required and called for at any time, being the only means of settling a dispute.

(c). The wholesale loss and waste of stores which has been going on for some time, is a matter which is now occupying the attention of Army and Corps Commanders. Strict orders have now been received that this is to be stopped. As a result of this the divisional commander directs that all losses of stores which cannot be satisfactorily accounted for, will be paid for by the units concerned.

2. Whenever the division takes over from another division the following procedure will be carried out.

(a). Lists of stores handed over (in duplicate) will be prepared - one copy will be given to the incoming unit, the other will be retained.
Lists are to be signed by representatives of the outgoing and incoming units.

(b). As to whether lists are made out by companies or battalions is a matter for units to arrange, but a collated list is to be sent to Divisional Headquarters as soon as possible after the relief is completed by -

    i   Infantry Brigades.
    ii   C.R.A.
    iii C.R.E.
    iv   A.D.M.S.
    v   A.D.V.S.
    vi   Camp Commandant D.H.Q.
    vii Pioneer battalions.
    viii Divisional Train.
    ix   Officer i/c Baths & Laundries.

3. The identical procedure is to be followed in the case of brigade reliefs within the division.

4. Neither Trench nor Camp Stores are to be removed by units no matter whether they are taken over by a unit or issued to it while in occupation.

F.C. Dundas.
Lt. Col.,
A.A. & Q.M.G., 20th Division

6/5/16

S E C R E T.   20th Division
                C/20/3842

ADMINISTRATIVE INSTRUCTIONS
in connection with relief of 20th Division
by 6th Division
----

1.   BILLETS -
        With reference to Operation Order No. 66 dated
9th July, para: 6. Other units will billet as shewn
on attached Appendix A.

2.   DIVISIONAL BATHS & LAUNDRY -
        The Divisional Baths and Laundry (RUE d'YPRES) will
be handed over on the 15th.
        The Laundry in RUE REMINGHELST will remain in
possession of the 20th Division.
        The Baths and Laundries at WORMHOUDT and ZEGGERS
CAPPEL will be taken over by 20th Division on the 14th.
        One N.C.O., and 4 men will be sent on by the 6th
Division and 1 N.C.O., and 6 men by the 20th Division on
the 13th inst., respectively. The Officer i/c Baths of
each Division will arrange accordingly.

3.   The Corps will be asked to change railheads on
the 17th.

4.   The Soldiers Home in POPERINGHE Square will be
handed over on the 15th. The Rev. James will arrange
to take over the one at WORMHOUDT on the 14th.

5.   The Divisional Armourer's Shop and Stores will be
exchanged on the 15th.

6.   The A.P.Ms. of the two Divisions will arrange a
date on which to hand over all the road control posts.

7.   Caretakers of P. & L. Posts will be relieved on
14th. D.A.Q.M.G., to arrange.

8.   The Officer Commanding Divisional Train will
arrange with O.C., 6th Divisional Train the dates on
which he will vacate his present lines and move to back
area. Dates selected to be reported to A.A. & Q.M.G.
        Supply waggons of Field Companies and Field
Ambulances will be attached to and remain with the A.S.C.
Company billeted nearest to these units.
        The supply wagons of R.A. units will either remain
with 158th Company at WORMHOUDT or be attached to and
remain with the A.S.C. Company at BOLLEZEELE, according
to whichever is nearest by road to the Artillery brigade
to which they are affiliated.

9.   A Table of Refilling Points will be issued in
Divisional Orders later.

10.   The 32nd Mob. Vet. Section will exchange billets with
the Mob. Vet. Section, 6th Division, on the 17th inst.

                                J. C. Dumas
                                    Lt. Col.,
11.7.16.   A.A. & Q.M.G., 20th Division.

Copies to -
6th Div.   C.R.A.   61st Bde   A.D.V.S.   32nd M.Vet.   S.C.F.(C/E
G.S.   C.R.E.   D.L.I.   A.P.M.   Sec.   S.C.F.(R.C
A.A. & Q.M.G.   Signals.   Div.Trn.   S.S.O.   Baths.   S.C.F.(Wes
D.A.L. & Q.M.G. 59th Bde   M.S.C.   Camp Cmdt   Salvage Co.
D.A.Q.M.G.   60th Bde   A.P.M.S.   33rd San.Sec. Town Major
                                                      POP

S E C R E T

APPENDIX. A.

20th Division
C/20/3842

Reference Operation Order 66, Units will occupy billets as under while in Corps Reserve.

H.Q., & 158th Coy. A.S.C.	(¼ WORMHOUDT (¾ BOLLEZEELE.
159th Coy. "	WORMHOUDT.
160th Coy. "	BOLLEZEELE.
161st Coy. "	WATOU.
A. Coy., R.E.	WINNEZEELE.
B. Coy., R.E.	HOUTKERQUE.
11th D.L.I.	WINNEZEELE.
33rd Sanitary Sect:	WORMHOUDT (same billets as before)
32nd Mob. Vet. Sect:	C.27.a.6.4.
Div. Armourer's Shop	ESQUELBECQ.
D.A.D.O.S. Stores	ESQUELBECQ.
Salvage Coy.	ESQUELBECQ.
Divisional Band.	ESQUELBECQ.

S E C R E T.

O.C. 83rd Company R.E.

O.C. 96th Company R.E.

    For your information and return by last named. Please pass quickly.

    Units will move in accordance with the attached programme, and Disposition Reports will be wired to this office as usual, as soon as possible after completion of move.

    C.R.E's Office will be closed in POPERINGHE at 8 a.m. on 16th instant and reopened at ESQUELBECQ at 3 p.m. the same day.

12th July, 1916.

                                        Captain R.E.
                          for   C.R.E. 20th Division.

SECRET

O.C. 83rd Field Co, R.E.

Herewith copy of detailed moves
of Cos of 6th Divn, for your
information

11.7.16

J. Masse
CAPTAIN. R.E.
ADJUTANT R.E. 20th DIVISION

COMMANDING ROYAL ENGINEERS
No. ZH1858
11 JUL 1916
20th (LIGHT) DIVISION

Reference enclosed Programme of Reliefs between 20th and 6th Div:

1. No R.E. work on night of 15/16 on Left Sector. 3 Sections of 96th Co march from YPRES to H.7.a.5.9. after arrival of 12th Co, who should march down in small parties, so as to arrive in YPRES by 9.p.m. on 15th, at which hour O.C.96th Co hands over responsibility.

2. No R.E. work on night of 16/17 on Right Sector. 3 Sections 83rd Co hand over as in (1), but on 16/17 to London Coy being relieved of responsibility also at 9.p.m.

3. No Pioneer work on night of 15/16. Advance parties of 11th Leicesters to take over YPRES billets by 9.p.m., when 11th D.L.I. 2 Coys will march back, crossing the Co 11th Leicesters marching to YPRES.

4. 1 Co, 11th Leicesters in YPRES work, the 3 back Coys do not work that night.

Notes

Field Companies will send advance parties of Officers and men to the Companies from whom they are taking over works, at least two days before their respective reliefs take place.

It is unavoidable that
(a) The London Co will have 2 Sections bivouacking in 84th Co billet from 12/13 to 15/16.
(b) The 2/2 West Riding Co billet on night of 15/16 in field with H.Q. & 2 Sections 12th Co, at HOUTKERQUE.
(c) The 2/2 West Riding Co bivouac on night of 16/17 in billet of 83rd Co till that Co moves on the following day.

RELIEF OF 20th DIVISIONAL ENGINEERS BY 6th DIVISIONAL ENGINEERS.

UNIT.	Nights of:-						
	11th - 12th	12th - 13th	13th - 14th	14th - 15th	15th - 16th	16th - 17th	17th - 18th
84th (reserve) Co.		A.28.d.6.2.	A.28.d.6.2.	A.28.d.6.2.	A.28.d.6.2.	Not known.	"2 Secns. YPRES. H.8.a.5.9. G.12.d.5.3.
2/2 W. Riding. Reserve Co.				Volkeringhove	Houtkerk.	H.8.a.5.9 & G.12.d.5.3	H.Q. & 2 Sec.
1/1 London Fd.Co. Right Sector.	2 Secs. Ilver- dinghe, H.Q. & 2 Secns. at Lederinghem.	2 Sec. A.28 d.8.2. H.Q. & 2 Sec. Lodering- hem.	A.28.d.3.2 & 2 Sec. Lederinghem.	A.28.d.8.2 & Ledringhem.	A.28.d.8.2.	2 Sec. YPRES 2 Sec. H.Q. & 2 Sec. Houtkerk. (2)	2 Sec. YPRES H.Q. & 2 Sec. A.28.d.8.2.
83rd (Right Sector).					3 Sec. YPRES H.Q. & 1 Sec. H.8.a.5.9. & G.12.d.5.3.	Houtkerk.
12th (Left Sector.)	2 Sec. L.8. H.Q. & 2 Sec. 5.9.H.Q. & 2 Sec. & Houtkerk.	2 Sec. H.7.a. H.7.a.5.9. 5.9.H.Q. & 2 Sec. & Houtkerk.	H.7.a.5.9. Houtkerk.	H.7.a.5.9	2 Sec. YPRES H.8.a.5.9. H.Q. & 2 Sec. at H.7.a.5.9. K.12.c. Sheet 27.	2 Sec. YPRES H.Q. & 2 Sec. H.7.a.5.9. Houtkerk.
96th (Left Sector).	3 Sec. YPRES. H.Q. & 1 Sec H.7.a.5.9.	3 Sec YPRES H.Q. & 1 Sec H.7.a.5.9.				
11th D.L.I. Pioneers.			2 Cos. YPRES. H.Q. & 2 Cos. Brandhoek.	2 Cos. Brand- hoek. H.Q. & 2 Cos. "L" Poperinghe.	Brandhoek.	Winnezeele	Winnezeele
11th Leicesters. Pioneers.					Co. YPRES. H.Q. & 2 Co. at "L". (3) Brandhoek. Poperinghe.	1 Co. YPRES. H.Q. & 3 Cos. Brandhoek. Esquelbecq.	2 Cos. YPRES. H.Q. & 2 Cos. Brandhoek.
H.Q.R.E., 20th Divn.					Poperinghe.	Esquelbecq.	Poperinghe.
R.Q.R.E. 6th Divn.				Esquelbecq.	Esquelbecq.	Poperinghe.	Poperinghe.

Lieut.-Colonel,
C.R.E., 6th Division.

10th July, 1915.

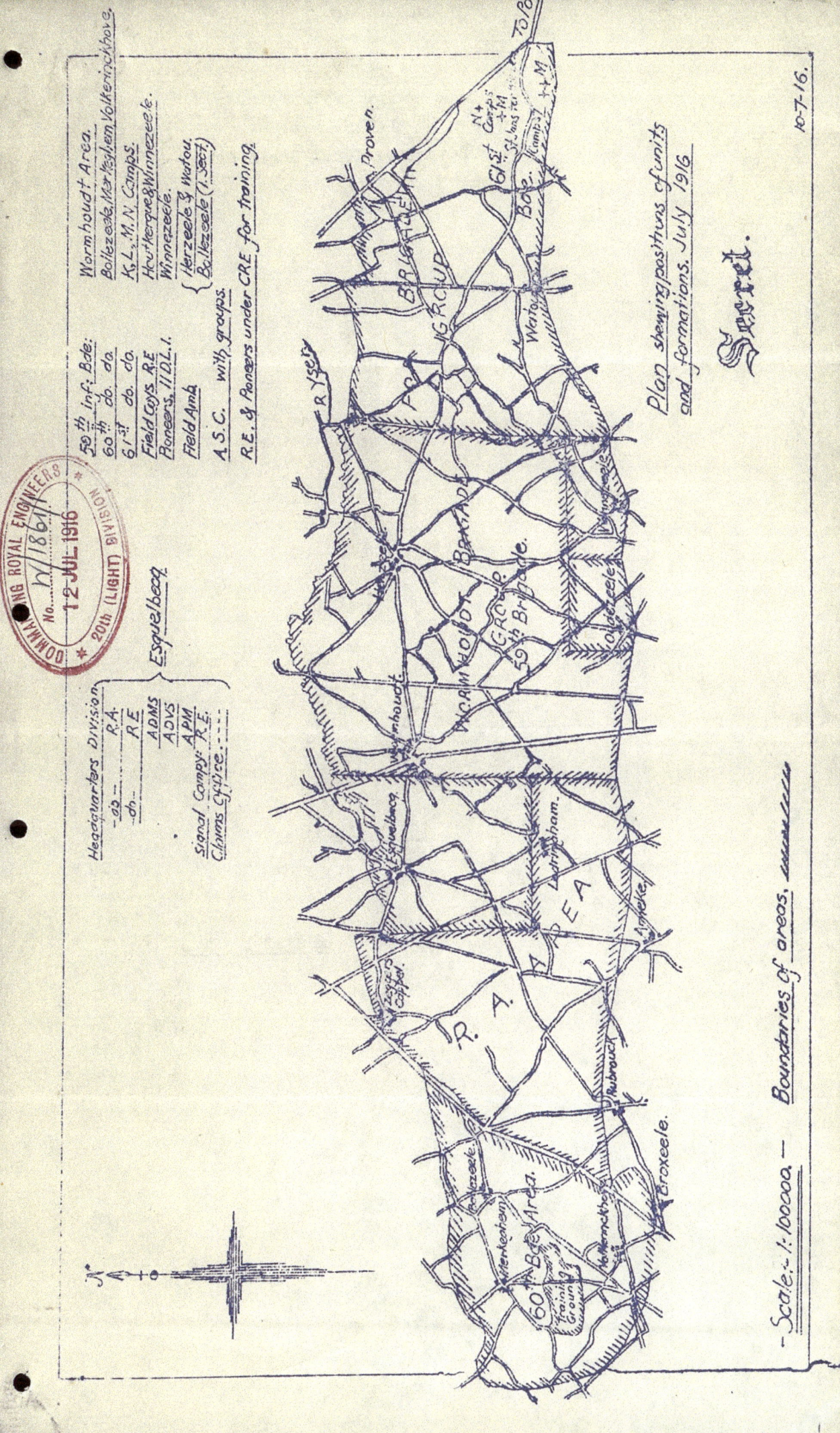

20th Divisional Engineers.

C. R. E.

20th DIVISION

AUGUST 1 9 1 6

No. 20
SECRET
C.R.E. Vol 14
Army Form C. 2118.

Hd Qrs R.E.
16 Divn.

WAR DIARY
or
INTELLIGENCE SUMMARY.
(Erase heading not required.)

Instructions regarding War Diaries and Intelligence Summaries are contained in F. S. Regs., Part II. and the Staff Manual respectively. Title pages will be prepared in manuscript.

Place	Date	Hour	Summary of Events and Information	Remarks and references to Appendices
COUIN (LENS?)	August 1		Divisional Front runs from K.17 a.1.5 North of HEBUTERNE to Q.4.6 S.E. 57° 60' + 21° Bde in the line with 96", 83", 86" Field Cos affiliated to them respectively. Most important work reducing trenches rendered unsafe by heavy shell fire during previous operations; preparing for attack by making suf. dugouts + heavy trench mortar emplacements.	
	6.		86" Field Coy relieves & hands over work in Right sector to 96" Coy of 15" Divn.	
	7.		83" F. Coy forms Coy in reserve moves into back billets at COIGNEUX.	
	10.		150" J. Coy of 15" Divn attached to 26" Divn for work. Major LE HOPKINS orders to proceed + take over as C.R.E. 37" Divn. Capt PENNYCUICK from ESTAPLAIRES	
			Major HOPKINS.	
	15.		130" J. Coy 15" Divn lent for work released to reyoin their Divn.	
	15.		Divn reld repeatedly released by Guards Divn + move to rear area.	
	16.		83" J.Coy march from COURCELLES to AMPLIER & bivouacs until 60" Bde.	
	17.		83" " " " THIÈVRES. 76" J. Coy to BOIS de WARNIMONT 4" Bde to BEAUVAL (that)	
BEAUVAL (Start) (ALBERT)	18.		84" J. Coy. march to HEM. 96" J. Coy. to BEAUVAL. 83" Coy. to ST HILAIRE.	
	19.		transport of J" Co marched up ? los 83" Coy & VILLERS BOCAGE along 15".	

1577   Wt. W10791/1773   500,000   1/15   D. D. & L.   A.D.S.S./Forms/C. 2118.

H.Q.R.E.
2nd Divn.

SHEET 2

WAR DIARY
or
INTELLIGENCE SUMMARY.
(Erase heading not required.)

Army Form C. 2118.

SECRET

Place	Date	Hour	Summary of Events and Information	Remarks and references to Appendices
TREUX (Sheet ALBERT)	20.		Dismantled nearly J.R.Cos & returned and marched off Lines 96"F.Co. at CANDAS fm. MERICOURT & marched to MEAULTE. 54" F.Co. will to MORLANCOURT. 63" F.Co. will & marched to VILLE SUR ANCRE. H^rs Qrs RE move to TREUX.	
	21.		Gnrl Hd move into H^r Crs Power. 53rd Jn Cy at SAND PITS. 54" F.Co. at H.Q.R.E.	
FORKED TREE 22. (L.2.h.9. Sheet ALBERT)			HAPPY VALLEY. 96" F.Co. at THE CITADEL. H^rs Qrs RE. FORKED TREE. Commence relief of 20" Divn. 83rd F.Co. less transport move to CARNOY + take over from 129"Army Co. 96" F.Co. less transport move to 11 CRATERS (F.12.c.6.9.) + take over from 106" F.Co. 96" Field Cy less transport move to CARNOY and take over from 103" F.Co. Transport of F.Cos at SAPPER CORDER BRAY.	
Advanced H^r Qrs. 23.			95" F.Co. affiliated for work to 35" Bde; 51" F.Co. to 6" Bde. 83rd F.Co. in reserve.	
H^r Qrs (F.18 Sheet ALBERT) 26. 27.			Work mostly necessary trenches & mostly made, also close up of N & of GUILLEMONT. 4"Battalion Grleston Guard attacked 6.20 Pm & took 61" Bde + 54" F.Co. to reserve, relieved by 61" Bde + 53" F.Co. respectively. nr. CLOVER wooden hut and dug-out wire trenches close to GUILLEMONT.	
	28.		Moved to continued storing matter necessary to various areas to self all work in trenches on works &c.	

21-8-16.

20th Divisional Engineers

C. R. E.

20th DIVISION

SEPTEMBER 1 9 1 6

Appendices attached;- Report on Capture of GUILLEMONT

Army Form C. 2118

Hqrs. RE "26" Divn

WAR DIARY
or
INTELLIGENCE SUMMARY.
(Erase heading not required.)

SECRET

Vol 15

Place	Date	Hour	Summary of Events and Information	Remarks and references to Appendices
Sheet ALBERT. 57/51-F.19. MINDEN POST.	1st		Issued C.R.E. Operation Order No. 6. (with Operation "A") reference attack on 5th Bn/5t. 20th Divn to capture GUILLEMONT. 96th F Coy + M.T. Coy 11th D.L.I. Pioniers placed at disposal of 59th Bde. 83rd Fd Coy + one Coy D.L.I. at disposal of 41st Bde of Bn's attached to 20th Divn.	
	3rd		Stop of attack on GUILLEMONT. attack very successful. fine relief of Sappers + Pioniers work. Sevir in attacked offensive A.	
CORBIE.	6th		H.Q. R.E. march fm MINDEN POST to CORBIE. 82nd Field Cy march to SANDPITS near MEAULTE - 96th Field Cy march to BRAY. 83rd Field Cy march to VAUX-SUR-SOMME.	
	8th		83rd Field Cy march to VAUX-SUR-SOMME. 82nd march to MERICOURT L'ABBE. 96th Field Cy to CORBIE.	
	9th		96th F.C. march to bivouac at VAUX-SUR-SOMME. also 76th F.C. for pontoon practice.	
	10th		83, 96 + 76 Field Co's practised and attacked by Genl. 20 "Divn" who complimented them on their excellent work	
FORKED TREE CAMP. L26 a9.	11th		83rd Field Cy march to MEAULTE - 82nd F.C. to MERICOURT L'ABBE - 96th F.C. to BOIS de TAILLES. HqRs RE march to FORKED TREE CAMP.	
	12th		96th F.Cy march to SANDPITS.	

SHEET 2.   H.Q. 2nd
            20th Divn

Army Form C. 2118.

WAR DIARY   SECRET
    or
INTELLIGENCE SUMMARY.

(Erase heading not required.)

Instructions regarding War Diaries and Intelligence
Summaries are contained in F. S. Regs., Part II.
and the Staff Manual respectively. Title pages
will be prepared in manuscript.

Place	Date	Hour	Summary of Events and Information	Remarks and references to Appendices
	14"		83rd Fd Coy moved to CITADEL also 5th Coy. 96th Field Coy moved to BILLON FARM - F30a. 61st Bde Group including 94th Field Coy placed under orders of Comdg. Guards Division. E" Bde Group ordered to attack the Quad on their left & 6th Divn on their right	
	15"		94th Fd Coy moved to TALUS BOIS thro' 6 WATERLOT FARM in reserve to Guards Divn at C.13b. 83rd Fd Coy moved to TALUS BOIS 96th Fd Coy moved to TALUS BOIS A15a.	
	16"		6th Bde attacked & reached first objective Zenith Trench T9a 6.7 & T9 b.4.9. but as 6th Divn & Guards Divn on their right & left respectively were held up they consolidated. 94th Field Coy made strong points on both flanks. 83rd Field Coy with 60th Bde ordered the "Field Coy with 61st Bde in front line 96th Fd Coy with 59th Bde relieved 3rd Guards Bde. Very wet & stormy night. For the Divn took over line from Leuze Wood. CRE moved to Carnoi Brie H.Q.	
	17"		at 6am at BERNAFAY WOOD. H.Qrs RE Establishment transferred to MINDEN POST 83rd & 96th Field Coys assisted in consolidating line held. Assembly trench from T9a 39 via T9 a 9.6 T9 b. 4.5 dug by 83rd 94th & 96th Field Coys, relieved by XI. D.L.I. Pioneers.	
MINDEN POST	18/9.			

SHEET 3.   H.Q. R.E. 10 Divn.

Army Form C. 2118.

WAR DIARY
or
INTELLIGENCE SUMMARY.
(Erase heading not required.)

SECRET

Place	Date	Hour	Summary of Events and Information	Remarks and references to Appendices
	20"		Divn. relieved by Guards Divn. 96" Field Coy marched to Sandpits near MEAULTE.	
	21"		H.Q. Divn. R.E. march to FORKED TREE CAMP.	
TREUX	22"		H.Q. Divn R.E. march to TREUX. 93" & 81" F.Cos. march to TREUX & MEAULTE respectively.	
	23"		96" Field Coy marched to MORLANCOURT.	
	25"		Our. Solin R.E. f.C. sent to look at roads under C.E. 14" Corps.	
			81" Field Coy marched to CITADEL. 96" F. Coy marched to HAPPY VALLEY L5a7.7.	
	26"		81" F.Coy marches to MALTZHORN VALLEY S30s.	
	27"		81" F.Coy marched to CARNOY. H.Qrs R.E. moved to new Divi H.Qrs at A4 d.4.2 at 10 a.m. 93"d F. Coy marched to TRONES WOOD.	
FORKED TREE	28"		96" Field Coy marched to TALUS BOIS A15a. H.Qr. R.E. marched to FORKED TREE CAMP at 10 a.m. on relief by 2nd French Divn.	
	29"		81" F. Coy has H.Qrs Transport Horses & LONGUEVAL S16 E.2. preparatory to taking over from R.E. of 62nd Inf. Bde. C.R.E. went to recce Divn H'Qrs at BERNAFAY WOOD at 3 p.m.	

Maxwell C.O.S.R.E.
H.C.R.E. 11 Divn.

APPENDIX A. WAR DIARY

R.E. Report on the capture of GUILLEMONT.

Disposition before the attack.

The accompanying plan marked "A" shows the disposition of the troops, including the R.E. & Pioneers, before the attack. The 96th & 83rd Companies R.E. each with one Company D.L.I. (Pioneers) were placed at the disposal of G.O.C. 59th (Right) and 61st (Left) Brigades respectively. The 84th Coy R.E. with two Companies D.L.I. remained in Divisional Reserve.

Summary of Orders given to R.E. Companies & Pioneers.

The G.O.C. 59th Bde ordered the O.C. 96th Coy to follow up the attacking columns as soon as the first objective was reached & to make strong points; to detail ½ section R.E. and 1 section Pioneers for each of 6 strong points in the various objectives, those detailed for points in the 2nd & 3rd objectives pushing forward from the 1st objective as the others were taken. Also as soon as strong points were done to connect by a C.T. the 3rd objective, i.e., East side of GUILLEMONT back to old front line.

The G.O.C. 61st Bde ordered the O.C. 83rd Coy. R.E. to send up with the assaulting columns small parties of 2 to 4 men for each selected strong point to assist the Infantry at these points and parties of 20 Infantry were detailed for work at each strong point; the O.C. 83rd Coy. R.E. to send forward more R.E. with D.L.I. to work on the strong points as soon as opportunity offered. Also as soon as the strong points were done to connect by a C.T. the 3rd objective, i.e., East side of GUILLEMONT back to the old front line.

The C.R.E. ordered the 84th Coy R.E. and two Companies D.L.I. (Pioneers) to stand fast on the west edge of BERNAFAY wood till 5.30 p.m., when they were to carry up wiring material to the final objective then reached, the 84th Coy R.E. to wire that objective and the D.L.I. to there endeavour with 1 Company to clear a German C.T. which ran parallel to the GUILLEMONT - COMBLES Road and about 150ˣ north of it, back from the GINCHY - MAUREPAS Road towards GUILLEMONT, and to, if possible

possible, connect it with a trench to be dug by the other company from the GRIDIRON Trenches at about T.19.a.5.6 to N.E. corner of GUILLEMONT and on towards T.19 central.

The work done is shown on the accompanying plan marked "B" and was for the most part exactly as ordered, except that connection was not established between the old German C.T. from about T.20.c.1.7. to T.19. central, as this C.T. did not extend nearly as far back as was expected.

Rain and weather conditions made work extremely difficult. The 83rd and 96th Companies, with the Company of D.L.I. Pioneers attached to each, improved and wired the hasty defences begun on the previous night, and carried up the strong points on East side of GUILLEMONT to make a continuous line and went on with the C.T.s back from East of GUILLEMONT to the old front line.

The 2 Companies D.L.I. in reserve were detailed to occupy a portion of the line on 59th Bde. front.

The 2. Coy R.E. was ordered to establish at strong points on the 4th final objective line from westernmost corner of LEUZE wood to T.20.a.6.5. These to include one at the small quarry in T.20.c., one across the road at about T.20.d.3.6 one at T.20.a.6.5 and one about half way between the latter two. This work to be done directly after the strong patrols had pushed out to the 4th objective. No infantry being available and the R.E. sections being much reduced very little was done; one section made a very small point just behind the quarry; two others dug three small points (one in the road and one on either side of the road) but only about half way between 3rd & 4th objectives, & the other 4th section one at about T.20.a.3.2. only about 50 yds in front of the 3rd objective. The reason for these small points being dug so much further back than intended on the left was that the enemy had dug a line across about T.20.a.4.4 in a S.E. direction towards the road.

Work done on 3rd/4th

Work done on 4th/5th

General Remarks

Capt. J.A.C. PENNYCUICK, R.E., the O.C. 85th Company R.E. made a day and night reconnaissance of the Northern half of GUILLEMONT on 3rd and gives an opinion that one of the main causes of the rapid capture of GUILLEMONT, was the attack from the GRIDIRON on the North side. The GRIDIRON assembly trenches had been dug the 2 or 3 nights previous to the attack; the LEINSTER Battalion of the 47th Brigade occupied them before dawn on 3rd, and the discipline of this Battalion in crouching, crowded, in them for some seven hours without exposing themselves, is worthy of special mention; their attack from this side came as a surprise, and the German line on the North side of GUILLEMONT was at once captured and it was found that the enemy had several machine guns in this line facing Southwards; it is more than probable that these machine guns had caught troops in previous attacks as they swept across GUILLEMONT from the West side going Eastward.

The importance of not consolidating on a line like the edge of a wood or a village was once more established.

Had the line along the 2nd Objective been on the road marking the Eastern edge of the village, casualties would have been very heavy as this edge was repeatedly barraged; the line was placed 30 yds behind the road on the left and 100 yds or so in front on the right; the casualties were extraordinarily few on that line.

Employment of R.E.

Judging by results I do not think any improvements can be suggested. The 96th Coy had all its men in at a very early stage, which probably accounts for their casualties being heavier than in the other companies. The 85th Coy sent 2 to 4 men with each party of 20 Infantry detailed to establish strong points. Half the Company going up when opportunity offered, arrived at the Eastern edge,

edge of GUILLEMONT at 7.30 p.m. and worked on the strong points already started, whilst the other half of this company relieved them at 10 p.m.

The strong points consisted of small lengths of trench with flanks set back and two open machine gun emplacements in each. They varied in size, being for a garrison of anything from half to one platoon. To a considerable extent the strong points were connected together, sometimes by R.E. & Pioneers and sometimes by Infantry.

The handling of each of the three Field Companies by the Officers Commanding, the devotion to duty shown by them, the officers and all ranks under them left nothing to be desired.

The 11th D.L.I. (Pioneer) was split up into companies & here again one and all worked with great zeal and devotion to duty.

The following is a total list of the 20th Divn R.E. casualties during the GUILLEMONT operations:—

Casualties R.E.

Unit	OFFICERS			OTHER RANKS			Total Officers	Total O.R.	Total all ranks
	Killed	Wounded	Missing	Killed	Wounded	Missing			
83rd Field Coy.	—	1	—	2	4	3	1	12	13
84th Field Coy.	—	2	—	—	16	1	2	17	19
96th Field Coy.	—	2	—	5	32	2	2	39	41
Total	—	5	—	7	55	6	5	68	73

8th Sept 1916.

H. Holland
Lieut. Col. R.E.
C.R.E. 20th Division

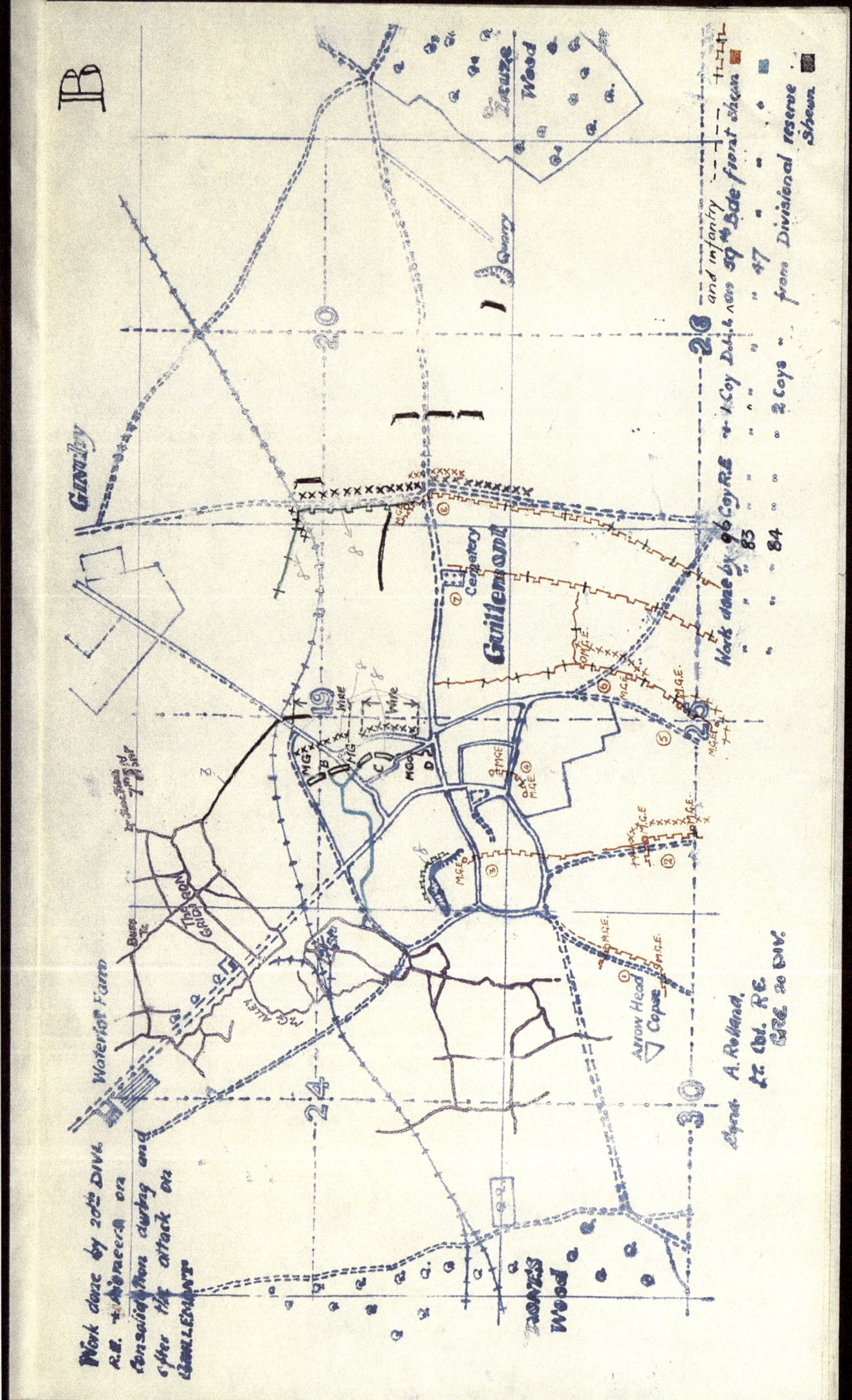

20th Divisional Engineers

C. R. E.

20th DIVISION

OCTOBER 1 9 1 6

Vol 16

20 Division

SECRET
H.Q. R.E.
20ᵗʰ Divn.

WAR DIARY
or
INTELLIGENCE SUMMARY
(Erase heading not required.)

Army Form C. 2118.

Instructions regarding War Diaries and Intelligence Summaries are contained in F. S. Regs., Part II. and the Staff Manual respectively. Title pages will be prepared in manuscript.

Place	Date	Hour	Summary of Events and Information	Remarks and references to Appendices
BERNAFAY WOOD S.28.B.5.6 Sheet 57ᵈ S.W.	October 1916 1/10/16		H.Q.R.E. with 20ᵗʰ Divn HQ at S.28.B.5.6.	
			N.27.c.4.9 & N.33.B.6.5. 83ʳᵈ Company in the line with 60ᵗʰ Brigade between 83ʳᵈ Company & 96ᵗʰ Brigade	A.E.
	2–3ʳᵈ		83ʳᵈ Company & 84ᵗʰ Company in the line with 60ᵗʰ Brigade between from 84ᵗʰ Company with 60ᵗʰ Brigade in close support and 96ᵗʰ Company with 59ᵗʰ Brigade in reserve. 84ᵗʰ Company supplied in the line, 83ʳᵈ Company & 96ᵗʰ on forming dumps of R.E. Material at GUILLEMONT and at S.24.7.8.8., also improving track from TRONES wood to N.E. of GUINCHY & from GUINCHY to N.W. T.1, and dug out at T.8. central for signals.	H.E. A.E. A.E.
	4ᵗʰ		Do on 1ˢᵗ	
	5–6ᵗʰ		59ᵗʰ Brigade + 96ᵗʰ Company relieved 61ˢᵗ Brigade with 84ᵗʰ Company in the line ; 84 & 96 Companies exchanged duties Do on 4ᵗʰ	A.E. A.E.
	7ᵗʰ		61ˢᵗ Brigade with 84ᵗʰ Company + 60ᵗʰ Brigade with 83ʳᵈ Company relieved left + right half of line occupied by 59ᵗʰ Brigade + attacked + obtained their objective (CLOUDY TRENCH) but had to withdraw their flank owing to failure of both 6ᵗʰ Division on right + left. 84 + 83ʳᵈ Companies consolidated the line gained 96ᵗʰ Company dug a C.T. from old to new front.	A.E. A.E.
	8ᵗʰ 9ᵗʰ		Brigade in the line with associated Companies relieved by Brigade of 6ᵗʰ Division. Division relieved by 6ᵗʰ Division + 20ᵗʰ Divn. H.Q. moved back to TREUX. 96ᵗʰ Company to VILLE SUR ANCRE with 59ᵗʰ Brigade, 83ʳᵈ + 84ᵗʰ Field Companies with bns of 60ᵗʰ Brigade to F.19. central (ALBERT map 1/40,000) + MÉAULTE respectively.	A.E. A.E.
	10–14ᵗʰ		Rested	
	15ᵗʰ		83ʳᵈ + 84ᵗʰ Companies with bns of 60ᵗʰ Brigade moved to DAOURS + CORBIE. Divl H.Q. with H.Q.R.E. from TREUX to CORBIE.	H.E.

1577 Wt. W10791/1773 500,000 1/15 D. D. & L. A.D.S.S./Forms/C.2118.

WAR DIARY
or
INTELLIGENCE SUMMARY.

(Erase heading not required.)

Page 2

Army Form C. 2118.

Place	Date	Hour	Summary of Events and Information	Remarks and references to Appendices
CORBIE	16-17ᵗʰ		Sheet 2	
A.8.a.	18ᵗʰ		Rested.	Ap
(ALBERT map 1/40,000)			20ᵗʰ Div. R.E. left its Division in rest & returned to A.8.a. for work on hutting in A.8.a. & water supply (Anft. Bn.)	Ap
	19ᵗʰ–24ᵗʰ		near BERNAFAY WOOD under C.E. XIV Corps.	Ap
			As in 18ᵗʰ :-	
CONDE (S.W. corner of LENS map 1/40,000)	25ᵗʰ		H.Q. R.E. 920 "this" with 84ᵗʰ Company & recent draft, relieved by 23ʳᵈ 46ᵗʰ Company deprived 20ᵗʰ Division in rest area for purpose of training new draft; 83ʳᵈ 46ᵗʰ Companies remained at A.8.a. on hutting.	Ap
	26ᵗʰ to 31ˢᵗ		83ʳᵈ 46ᵗʰ Companies - less recent draft - remained at A.8.a. on hutting. Remainder of Divisional R.E., viz. H.Q., 84ᵗʰ Company + draft from 23ʳᵈ 46ᵗʰ training at CONDE.	Ap

O.Bernard Lt Col R.E.
C.R.E. 20ᵗʰ Div

31/10/16

20th Divisional Engineers.

C. R. E.

20th   DIVISION

NOVEMBER 1 9 1 6

SECRET. WAR DIARY H.Q. R.E. 20th Division. Army Form C. 2118.

or

~~INTELLIGENCE SUMMARY.~~

(Erase heading not required.)

Instructions regarding War Diaries and Intelligence Summaries are contained in F.S. Regs., Part II. and the Staff Manual respectively. Title pages will be prepared in manuscript.

Place	Date	Hour	Summary of Events and Information	Remarks and references to Appendices
	November 1916.			
CONDE. S.W. Corner of LENS 11 Map 1/40,000	1st to 7th		H.Q. R.E. and 84th Field Company R.E. with drafts from 83rd and 96th Field Companies continued training.	
	8th		Captain I.W. Massie, on return from leave, took over command of 83rd Field Company R.E., his appointment dating from 31/10/16.	
PICQUIGNY.	9th		H.Q. R.E., and 84th Field Company with drafts from 83rd and 96th Companies moved to PICQUIGNY. 84th Field Company and attached drafts continued training.	
	10th		2/Lieut: H.E. Hill, from 84th Company R.E., on return from leave, took over duties of Adjutant, his appointment dating from 31/10/16.	
	11th		83rd and 96th Field moved back from A.8.a (ALBERT Sheet) to billets in VILLE.	
	14th		84th Field Company R.E. moved to LALEU.	
CORBIE.	15th		H.Q. R.E. and 83rd Field Company R.E. moved to CORBIE. Detachments of 83rd and 96th Field Companies rejoined their respective companies. Lieut. Colonel A. Rolland took over temporary duty as Chief Engineer XIVth Corps, and Captain M.A.H. Scott those of C.R.E. 20th Division.	
	16th		83rd and 96th Companies working on stabling and hutting in Ville and Laundry and Stabling in CORBIE areas.	
	18th		84th Field Company moved to DAOURS.	
	19th		84th Field Company working on 17th, 20th and 29th Divisional Schools and R.A. School at DAOURS.	
	24th		Major P.F. Story R.E. returned from leave and took over duties of C.R.E. Captain M.A.H. Scott rejoined 84th Field Company R.E.	
	27th		84th Field Company R.E. moved to CITADEL (F.21. ALBERT), and 96th Field Company R.E. to DAOURS, leaving one section at TREUX.	
	28th		84th Field Company R.E. moved to MANSEL CAMP (F.11.c.8.8. - ALBERT) to work under orders of C.R.Es Guards and 29th Divisions.	
	28th to 30th.		96th Field Company R.E. working on Schools at DAOURS. 83rd Company continue working on stables and Laundry at CORBIE.	

[signature]
Major R.E.
a/C.R.E. 20th Division.

20th Divisional Engineers

C. R. E.

20th DIVISION

DECEMBER 1 9 1 6

SECRET.

WAR DIARY OF HEADQUARTERS ROYAL ENGINEERS, 20th DIVISION.

Army Form C. 2118.

(Erase heading not required.)

Instructions regarding War Diaries and Intelligence Summaries are contained in F.S. Regs., Part II. and the Staff Manual respectively. Title pages will be prepared in manuscript.

Place	Date	Hour	Summary of Events and Information	Remarks and references to Appendices
	DECEMBER 1916.			
CORBIE	1st		83rd Field Company R.E. continues on stables and laundry at CORBIE; 84th Company at work on MANSEL Camp and 96th Company on Schools at DAOURS.	
	2nd		C.R.E. returns from attachment to XIVth Corps. Major P.F. STORY rejoined 96th Company.	
	3rd/8th		Work continues as above.	
	9th		83rd removed to TREUX from CORBIE leaving one section at CORBIE.	
	10th		83rd and 84th removed to TRONES WOOD. 96th removed to TREUX from DAOURS.	
BRIQUETERIE	11th		H.Q.R.E. moved to BRIQUETERIE from CORBIE. 96th Company to BERNAFAY. Taking over line from N.34.b.9.9. to T.6.b.7.3. from 29th Division.	
	12th/22nd		Companies working on Strong Points, Intermediate line, maintenance and construction of Duckwalks, construction and repair of Dugouts &c.	
	23rd		96th Company to CORBIE. 84th Company to MEAULTE.	
	24th		83rd - Two sections CARNOY-MONTAUBAN Road. H.Q. and one section to BRONFAY FARM, joined by the section from CORBIE. 96th - one section to DAOURS.	
CORBIE.	25th		H.Q.R.E. move to CORBIE. Handed over to 17th Division.	
	26th/31st		Companies working on improvements to camps, hutting, railways sheds at MARICOURT, stables and Laundry at CORBIE &c.	

J.B.Sur
Lieutenant R.E.
for Commanding Royal Engineer, 20th Division.

WAR DIARY
of the
H.Q. R.E. 20th Division
January 1917

Vol 19

SECRET.

WAR DIARY
or
INTELLIGENCE SUMMARY.
(Erase heading not required.)

Headquarters R.E. 20th Division.

Army Form C. 2118.

Instructions regarding War Diaries and Intelligence Summaries are contained in F. S. Regs., Part II. and the Staff Manual respectively. Title pages will be prepared in manuscript.

Place	Date	Hour	Summary of Events and Information	Remarks and references to Appendices
SOMME FRONT.	January 1917.			
CORBIE.	1st.		H.Q. R.E. at CORBIE, 83rd Field Company R.E. working at Camps at CRATERS and BRONFAY FARM; 84th Field Company R.E. working on Camps at MEAULTE and Hangars at MORLANCOURT; 96th Field Company R.E. moved to CITADEL from CORBIE.	
	2nd.		83rd Company moved to WEDGE WOOD and took over from 55th Field Company R.E.; 84th Company moved to COMBLES (Headquarters and 3 sections) and WEDGE WOOD (1section and transport) and took over work from 76th Field Company R.E.; 96th Company moved to COMBLES (Headquarters and 3 sections) and WEDGE WOOD (1 section and Transport) and took over work from 75th Field Company R.E. Headquarters R.E. took over from Guards Division C.R.E. at ARROWHEAD COPSE.	
	3rd.		The following awards were made in the New Year's Honours list:-	
			Major P.F. Story, 96th Fd. Co: R.E.)	
			Major F.J.M. Stratton, 20th Sig: Co: R.E.) Awarded D.S.O.	
			Captain M.A.H. Scott, 84th Field Co: R.E.)	
			Captain A.G. Brace, 20th Sig: Co: R.E.)	
			2/Lieut H.Y.V. Jackson, 83rd Field Co: R.E.) Awarded Military Cross.	
	4th. 3rd to 26th		20th Division took over from Guards Division line between U.2.c.2.2. to U.20.b.3.2. Companies worked on Strong Points, Communication Trenches to front line, wiring Intermediate line and Reserve Line, Deep dugouts, improving billets and bunk accommodation and Boot exchange and Aid Post.	
	15th		Captain R.H. WARDE, 96th Field Company R.E. awarded Military Cross for services on 7th October, 1916, near GUEDECOURT.	
	20th to 26th		84th Company worked on new support line from BREAD Trench (U.20.b.8.9.) to CAMEL Trench(U.14.a.7.8	
	26th		84th Company relieved by 77th Field Co: R.E. and moved, Headquarters and 2 sections to GROVETOWN, 1 section to DAOURS and 1 section to MORLANCOURT.	
	27th		83rd Company relieved by 78th Field Co: R.E., moved to MEAULTE. 96th Co:, relieved by 93rd Co: moved to FRANVILLERS.	
	28th		H.Q.R.E. and 20th Division relieved by 17th Division, moved to Reserve Area with H.Q. at HEILLY. 83rd Co: moved to HEILLY.	
	29th		83rd Co: under Corps orders, working on 36 C.C.S., 84th Co: under Corps orders working on 34 C.C.S., XIVth Corps Rest Camp, Hangars and huts at MORLANCOURT and school at DAOURS. 96th Co: training.	

1577 Wt.W07291/1773 500,000 1/15 D.D.&L. A.D.S.S./Forms/C. 2118.

For C.R.E. 20th Division.
Lieutenant R.E.

HQ RE 20
Vol 20

WAR DIARY
or
INTELLIGENCE SUMMARY.
(Erase heading not required.)

Army Form C. 2118.

Place	Date	Hour	Summary of Events and Information	Remarks and references to Appendices
SOMME FRONT	FEBRUARY 1917		Reference Map ALBERT (continued) 1/2.0	
HEILLY	1		H.Q. R.E. at HEILLY, 83 FCRE at HEILLY working under XIV Corps on 36.39 C.C.S.	
			84 FCRE HQ and 2 sections at BRAYTOWN working under XIV Corps under on 34 C.C.S and Corps Rest Station. 1 section at 2 hours on roads, 1 section at MORLANCOURT working on hangars for 9th Squadron R.F.C. 96 FCRE at FRONVILLERS having cutting fascines and employing billets etc.	
	4		96 FCRE moved to MEAULTE. Worked on billets and company equipment	
	7		83 FCRE moved to TRONES WOOD (S.30.a) 9 relieved 453rd (W. Riding) FCM MONTH Scott	
	8		84 FCRE moved to BERNAFAY WOOD (S.29.c) 9 relieved 498 (Kent) FCM Renont	
	76		96 FCRE moved to TRONES WOOD (S.30.a) 9 relieved 510 (London) FCM Desrousseurs Scott	
	28		Companies worked on camps, water supply, Reg Stns, M.C. emplacements & Tench Tram Track. 84 FCRE Ring on Renont & supply D.O.R.E. for Rail Camps	
	9		H.Q. R.E. moved to BRIQUETERIE (A.E.d) Taking over from CRE 29th Div.	
			20 Division relieved 29th Division on left sector of Corps Front (C.2.c.6 - M.35.d.6)	
	10		84 FCRE relieved officer of FCRE in Normal Desert and Office became Divisional Company	
			1st R.W. FORMAT killed while taking to an advanced post.	
	28		Wood Ring carried on as before. No further alteration in positions. A Runay Ham cat 20 Feb	

WAR DIARY
or
INTELLIGENCE SUMMARY.

Army Form C. 2118.

CRG 20 pm Vol 2

Place	Date	Hour	Summary of Events and Information	Remarks and references to Appendices
SOMME FRANCE	MARCH 1917		Ref map 57.C.	
	1		H.Q R.E. AT D.H.Q. (Sheet 62c). Division holding line SAILLY(exclusive)-SAILLISEL(inclusive) 23 F.C. in reserve working on camps, 64 F.C. in forward area, working on dug-outs, R.E. emplacements and T.M. emplacement, 96 F.C in RANCOURT area working on R.E. emplacements and dead horse tracks and wiring in front	
	2		23 F.C. relieved 96 F.C in RANCOURT area, 96 F.C in reserve working on camps, baths & railway	
	5		20th Division relieved portion of 29th, extending its front to include the copse of four winds.	
	8		96 F.C. relieved 23 F.C. in RANCOURT area, 23 F.C. in reserve working on camps and railway	
	14		23 F.C. relieved 64 F.C. in MORVAL sector, 64 F.C. in reserve working lifting	
	15		First advance on 20th Divisional front	
	16		64 F.C. relieved 96 F.C. in RANCOURT sector, 96 F.C. working across copse known as Liouville Wood.	
	17		On section east of F3 & F4 F.C.C. attached to 59th and 61st Brigades of advancing Div. moved to MORVAL then 23 F.C. moved to TRANSLOY. Employed on road repairs wells and tracks. Road works. 23 F.C. moved to T.27 a7 (SAILLISEL map) employed as above on march 21st.	
	18		H.Q R.E. AND Division H.Q. moved to GUILLEMONT, division reached RANCOURT, cape cavalry Bois 20 Division relieved portion of Guards Division, extending its front to include villages 96 F.C. relieved by 14 F.C. at equancourt, returned to YTRES	
	23 24 30 31		23 F.C. at TRANSLOY 64 F.C. at RANCOURT 96 F.C. at YTRES Division holding a line in front of RUYAUCOURT, NEUVILLE, EQUANCOURT.	

H Eles Kell Lt col RE 20 Div

Vol 22

26th Divisional Engineers.

War Diary

for month of April 1917.

Army Form C. 2118.

WAR DIARY
or
INTELLIGENCE SUMMARY.
(Erase heading not required.)

Instructions regarding War Diaries and Intelligence Summaries are contained in F. S. Regs., Part II. and the Staff Manual respectively. Title pages will be prepared in manuscript.

Place	Date	Hour	Summary of Events and Information	Remarks and references to Appendices
SOMME FRONT.	APRIL 1917		REF MAP SHEET 57 C.	
	1		H.Q.R.E. in GUILLEMONT. 63 FCRE in LECHELLE. Before move to YTRES. 96 FCRE in ROCQUIGNY. Coys working on roads, clearing villages of mines and debris, filling water ponds	
	4		METZ-EN-COUTURE cleared. Section of 93rd F.C.R.E. took part and captured machine gun	
	6		Conference was officers of this sector. Engineer H.Q. & 16 Coys of 21st Divn.	
			Divnal front, on N. to 61st on right, 56 to R.52 in rear. 9th Army Corps Front	
			HAVRINCOURT WOOD. HQ continues in YTRES. FCRE now worked on and zones	
			through wood; also Div HQ and Div Staff shelter. Companies meanwhile reconnoitre work.	
	14		95th FCRE relieved 63 FCRE in left sector	
	19		25 FCRE relieved 96 FCRE in right sector	
	21		TRESCAULT occupied.	
	25		95 FCRE relieved officer in left sector. Divn H.Q. moved to LITTRE WOOD R 26 central	
	26		RE material reached ROCQUIGNY by Narrow gauge railway.	
	27		Divnal dumps RE material started at NEUVILLE.	
	28		Commenced a Trench System on zones of trench warfare.	

Honor Military Medals gun awarded to Br 44427. Sgt M. Bell. 49772 Spr. L. Hamilton. 48840 Hyfl F. Reed. 25/4/17.

[signature] Lt. Col.
C.RE.

1577 Wt. W10791/1773 300,000 1/15 D. D. & L.   A.D.S.S./Form/C. 2118.

War Diary.

of.

20th Divisional Engineers.

for Month of May, 1917.

WAR DIARY
or
INTELLIGENCE SUMMARY.
(Erase heading not required.)

Army Form C. 2118.

Place	Date	Hour	Summary of Events and Information	Remarks and references to Appendices
FAVREUIL and QUEANT SECTORS			Sheet 57C ref map	
	1		Div HQ & HQ RE in LITTLE WOOD. P.26 central. 24 FCRE on line in QUEANT sector in front of PRONVILLECOURT. 83 FCRE on right in front of METZ. Front line extending from Q.11.860 to R.32.C.24. Work consisting of digging trenches, wiring and deep dugouts. M.G. emplacements and strongpoints, also 23 FCRE relieved on night sector by 98 FCRE.	
	11		Work on trench system with front, support and reserve lines of trenches and were wired supports, shelters and M.G. emplacements, also communication supply. Divisional right boundary extended to R.14.d.2.0. Taking over from 229 FCRE 40 T Dennison. 83 FCRE worked on this sector on general trench system.	
	13		84 FCRE relieved on QUEANT by 427 FCTE of 42nd Division	
	19		98 - - 428 -	
	21		- centre - - -	
	22		- right - 429 -	
	23		Field companies moved by stages to line TEHAR C.20.a.25 - Q.23.C.80. HQRE moved to H.15.C. CRE 42nd Division taking over from CRE 20th 20th Divns. Left 1st Corps and 4th Army after 2 months with 1st Army and 9 months with Corps. Relief carried out during after Army Commander thanking	

WAR DIARY
or
INTELLIGENCE SUMMARY.
(Erase heading not required.)

Army Form C. 2118.

Place	Date	Hour	Summary of Events and Information	Remarks and references to Appendices
GUEANT	20th		Sheet 57 c. G. 51 F.	
			Reconn. for New Defences	
	21.		20 F.C.R.E. on recon. in new area, billets at H16 central, relieving 15th Berkshire	
			F.C. of 5th ANZAC Divison. 1 ANZAC Corps.	
	24.		96 F.C.R.E. relieve 1st F.C. Australian E. on right aera sect	
	25.		83 F.C.R.E. — " " " — " Left	
	26.		C.R.E. 20th Divon from C.R.E. 3rd Aus 2nd Divon. 1 ANZAC Corps. 3rd army	
			with H.Q.R.E. at H15 C. Conference concerning ordinary supports &	
			general defence works. 20th Division transferred to 8 Corps.	
	28		84 F.C.R.E. relieve 96 F.C.R.E. on right sector	
	31		Divison Tr 5th Army relieved by 3rd Army	
			Honours. Mentioned in Despatches May 1917. 2/Lt (a/Capt) T.P. SMITH, T.O. H/20	
			Staff Capt Major WILSON of 83 F.C.R.E. CSM. J. GREEN and Sapper F.N. GREEN	
			of 84 F.C.R.E., 63561 Spr Monaghan, J.B. 96 F.C.R.E + No 59566 Sgt S. Ross 202nd Divl Signl Co	
			Invl Decoration. Médaille Militaire. No H7321 La Cpl. M. O'Neill 2nd Divl Signl Co. 105	

B. Ellis Bell
Lt. R.E.
for CRE 20th Divn

Vol 24

War Diary
of
20th Divl Engineers.   HDQRS &
                      3 FLD. COYS
       for   DIV SIG COY
    June 1917.

WAR DIARY
or
INTELLIGENCE SUMMARY.
(Erase heading not required.)

Army Form C. 2118.

Place	Date	Hour	Summary of Events and Information	Remarks and references to Appendices
GUEANT SECTOR JUNE 1917			Ref. Maps Sheet 57c and LENS 11.	
	1		Div. H.Q & CRE at H15c near BAPAUME. Division holding front between D.20.a.2.5 and V.23.c.7.5.2. 84 FCRE in right sector, D.2 in Left with 96 FCRE in reserve, working on general defences, wiring, dugouts. M.G. emplacements and abri vault Eine.	
	5		96 FCRE relieved 03 FCRE on Left sector	
	13		03 FCRE relieved 84 FCRE on right sector	
	16		Major M.B.H. SCOTT M.C. R.E. proceeded to LONDON. Capt. BENJAMIN M.C. R.E. appointed to 84 FCRE once formed, with acting rank of Major	
	22		84 FCRE relieved 96 FCRE in Left sector. Lt. G.H. KOHE R.E. appointed 2nd in command of 84 FCRE with acting rank of Captain	
	24		96 FCRE relieved by 461st FCRE (T.F.)	
	25		03 FCRE relieved by 460 FCRE (T.F.) CSM GREEN of 96 FCRE appointed a/RSM of 20th Div. R.E. R.S.M. LYNDON who proceeded to base. 96 FCRE moved to GOMIECOURT	
	26		03 FCRE moved to ACHIET-LE-PETIT. Major F.M. STRATTON D.S.O. R.E. late O.C. 20th Signal C.R.E. joined XIX Corps as A.D.S.S.	

WAR DIARY
or
INTELLIGENCE SUMMARY.
(Erase heading not required.)

Army Form C. 2118.

Instructions regarding War Diaries and Intelligence Summaries are contained in F. S. Regs., Part II. and the Staff Manual respectively. Title pages will be prepared in manuscript.

Place	Date	Hour	Summary of Events and Information	Remarks and references to Appendices
	27		84 F.Coy relieved by 457 F.Coy (T.F)	
	28		84 F.Coy moved to BINNCOURT. Transport of 96 F.Coy moved to ACHEUX. Coy 62nd Division relieved Coy 20th Div. HQRS. 20th Div. moved to BERNAVILLE by Lorry. Transport of HQRS moved to ACHEUX.	
	29		96 F.Coy arrived at GORGES. Remainder of Coy from ACHIET-LE-GRAND. Transport by road from ACHEUX. 83 F.Coy Remainder moved to ACHEUX. HQRS Transport arrived at BERNAVILLE	
	30		80 F.Coy arrived at pumples. Remainder by rail. Transport by road. 84 F.Coy Transport moved to ACHEUX.	

H. Ellis Hill
Lt.Col.
for
C.R.E. 20th Div.

War Diary

of

20th Divisional Engineers.

for

July, 1917.

Vol 25

WAR DIARY
or
INTELLIGENCE SUMMARY.
(Erase heading not required.)

Army Form C. 2118.

Instructions regarding War Diaries and Intelligence Summaries are contained in F. S. Regs., Part II and the Staff Manual respectively. Title pages will be prepared in manuscript.

Place	Date	Hour	Summary of Events and Information	Remarks and references to Appendices
JULY 1917.			Before maps LENS 11 and HAZEBROUCK S.A. and PROVEN 27.9.28.	
	1		H.Q.R.E. with H.Q. Div. March to DOMART. 83 F.C.RE at CANAPLES, 96 F.C.RE and moved to BERNAVILLE from BAPAUME area, 95 F.C.RE at ST LEGER. Conference training G.O.C. 20 miles. Inspected 3 Field Companies.	
	5		3 Field Companies marched to LA CHAUSSÉE for London training.	
	9		3 Field Companies returned to billets in CANAPLES, BERNAVILLE and ST LEGER.	
	12,13			
	17		Lt Col P ROLLAND took up appointment of CRE IV Corps troops. DSO M.E.	
	18		Lt Col E.M NEWELL DSO RE attached CRE 20 Div, 2 i/c to Col P ROLLAND. CRE and Adjutant moved to PROVEN.	
	19		83 F.C.RE arrived in PROVEN and by train, went billets at E.17.d.6.3. 96 F.C.RE	
	20		Div. HQ & H.B.R.E. detachment arrived at PROVEN. 24 F.C.RE arrived in PROVEN	
	21		area by train. 84 F.C.RE billets at E.4.C.C.1, 95 F.C.RE billets at F.10.a.6.2 inspected in IV Corps area, linked 20 Division on 5th Army. Conference training, Army evacuated London of the front line system moved in	Hart 27
	27		Map square C. Hartz 7.8.14	Hart 28
	30	10.0 p.m.	63 F.C.RE. move to A 18 Infantry to work on artillery track to attached MG 83 x 96 F.C.RE working on artillery road from B.24 F.6.2 and canal	Hart 25
	31		to HUDDLESTONE ROAD C.13.C. H Echelon billets in CAMP 22 B.	

C.R.E., 20th Division No. 53.

To:- O.C.93rd Field Co., R.E.
     O.C.96th Field Co., R.E.

C.R.E's OPERATION ORDER NO.27.

1. 93rd and 96th Field Companies R.E. will move to CANADA FARM Area with 59th Infantry Brigade Group.
   Packs will be left in present billets, but ground sheets will be carried with the haversacks.

2. Pontoon equipment and personnel and transport not required for the work in hand will be left at present billets. Pontoon wagons will be taken to CANADA FARM.

3. Os.C. Field Coys. will arrange to ration their Companies and attached Infantry for two days in the forward area.

4. O.C. Field Companies will arrange to meet 10 wagons each at ONDANK Dump at 3.0 p.m. on 30th instant to supervise loading with tools and material in accordance with list which will be forwarded.
   They will arrange for the parking of these wagons at night. The wagons will proceed to the work with Field Coys unless otherwise ordered.

5. 2 Orderlies from H.Q.,R.E. will report to C.R.E. at his H.Q. in forward area at 3.0 a.m. on 31st instant.
   1 orderly each from 93rd and 96th Field Companies will report to C.R.E. at same place and time. They must have previously reconnoitred the route to BARD CAUSEWAY.

6. C.R.E. and Adjutant R.E. will be at CANDEW FARM, A.19.b.0.8.,Sheet 28 from 3.0 a.m. on 31st instant onwards.
   An Officer of 84th Field Co.,R.E. will be at H.Q.,R.E. PROVEN during absence of C.R.E. and Adjutant in forward area.

29/7/17.

                                                     Lieut: R.E.,
                                        for C.R.E., 20th Division.

Copies to:- O.C.84th Field Co., R.E.
           "G", 20th Division.
           C.E.,XIVth Corps.
           B.G.C.,59th Infantry Brigade.

AO Pg 20 D
Vol 26

War Diary.

CRE:
3rd Field Coy
11th Field Coy
16th Field Coy
Sig Coy

WAR DIARY
or
INTELLIGENCE SUMMARY
(Erase heading not required.)

Army Form C. 2118.

Place	Date	Hour	Summary of Events and Information	Remarks and references to Appendices
AUGUST 1917			Reference Maps Sheets 20, 27, 28.	
	1		Div H.Q. and H.Q. R.E. at PROVEN. 83 F Coy at 20/A.8.6, 84 F Coy 27/C.4.c.8.1, 96 F Coy 28/A.11.c.	O.O 27
			83 F Coy working on forward roads. 84 F Coy Island 58.V.(Mesh) Bow on right across L.C. Coy Farm (20/L.28.a.8.2 - 20 "Bar" Island 58.V.(Mesh) Bow on right across 123 md on right restored	O.O. 28
			V. 27. 0. 8. 6). 96 F Coy at 28/A.15.R. 83 FCoy relief 123 md on right restored	O.O 29
	6		Reliefs at 28/c.19.c, 84 F relieved 124 F on left section west Zillebeke at 28/c.19.c, 92 F relieved 131 F in reserve west Zillebe at 22/5.21.d.	
	7		Coys working on tracks and tramways and roads.	
	10		Personnel RE Dump transferred from ordnance (R.S.C. (Bush Dump) to Canal Bank at 28/B.14.d.)	
	11-14		Coys working on tracks, railways and tramways Bath Mounts & east of Ypres (Canal) I avoided Panama Bridge	
	15		Coys reported New OP.15 & O.P.16 noted & concrete shelter taken for Bde H.Q. Coys on attack attacked at 4.45 a.m successfully and started final shelter consisting of line 20/U.24.6.0.2. to 0.17.d.2.5 .. Laying down	O.O 30
	16		wire entrench and overhead lawnmowers. 83 F and 96 F Coys laid out lighting to STEENHEK and overhead lawnmowers. 83 F and 96 F Coys laid out lighting to place the infantry. W.O. & Sappers of 3 Coys tot 15 worked in conjunction w/armed font at 808 GTR. 3 below at O.P. on assembly point of road by 5.5. Rds increasing pieces officers and on 5 & worked by the field ampy of 1005 F/Pot. 2 men of 84 F Regt PAY being badly sympathy section some a ppr worker to field guns area 07-ESH-528	

WAR DIARY or INTELLIGENCE SUMMARY

Army Form C. 2118.

Place	Date	Hour	Summary of Events and Information	Remarks and references to Appendices
PROVEN	1917 AUGUST 17		96th Coy. relieved by 124th Coy. Moved by rail to PROVEN area. 84 relieved by 157th Coy. Moved to Malarsie farm area 28/D.22.	
	18		84th Coy. move by rail to PROVEN area. 62nd Coy. relieved by 124th Coy. Moved to malakoff Fm.	
	19		20th Coy relieved by 96 Res. 62nd Coy moved by rail to PROVEN area	
	20		R.E. & N.S. hoste at PROVEN	
	21		Coys rapidly training & undertaking erection of rifle ranges.	
			84th Coy moved to miss'n farm 8.14.c 7.2. 2nd Lieut. Von Koch & new Bn H.Q.	
			96th Coy moved to 28/8.10d and undertook tunnel works	
			62nd Coy training	
			83rd Coy relieved 96th Coy at farmer area.	
	31		Casualties during period in 4 cad. jefasuden 6 Officers wounded (2 died o. w.) & other ranks (33 being off enough). 2 Officers and 17 O.R. wing gassed	
			By new weather at	
			Honors. 84th T.F.C.M.E. No 5364 U/Cpl v. KEECH. No 11896 St. J. WILSON.	
			20th Coy. and CRE No 57872 L/Cpl J. J. BAILEY No 2737 Spr. G. W. BONHAM.	
			No 4254 Spr. J. J. RYELL.	
			One sapper awarded the military medal	

H. Ellis Hill
Capt. R.E.
To CRE 201 Bde.

OPERATION ORDER NO. 28.

Copy No. 1

AA 54

by

C.R.E., 20th Division

Relief.

The Three Field Companies and the Pioneer Battalion of the 20th Division will relieve the Three Field Companies and Pioneer Battalion of the 38th Division on the morning of the 6th inst:

The 83rd Field Company R.E. will take over the quarters now occupied by the 123rd Field Company R.E. in the West Canal Bank at C.19.c.3.3. and Transport Lines at B.24.d.7.8.

The 84th Field Company R.E. will take over the quarters now occupied by the 124th Field Company R.E. in the West Canal Bank at C.19.c.2.6. and Transport Lines at B.24.d.7.4.

The 96th Field Company R.E. will take over the quarters now occupied by the 151st Field Company R.E. in the West Canal Bank at C.19.c.3.3. and Transport Lines at B.24.d.8.6.

The 11th Durham Light Infantry Pioneer Battalion will take over the quarters now occupied by the 38th Division Pioneer Battalion in the West Canal Bank at C.19.a.0.3.

The relief to be completed by 2.0. p.m. on the 6th inst:

Work on the new plank road over BARD CAUSEWAY and HUDDLESTON ROAD will be taken over by 38th Division on the 6th inst. The 20th Division will cease work on these roads on the evening of the 5th instant.

Advance Parties.

Units will send on advance parties to take over the quarters and work of the units they will relieve and will be prepared to carry on with the work they take over on the 6th inst.

Route.

The 83rd Field Company R.E., 96th Field Company R.E. and the 11th D.L.I.Pioneer Battalion must march by the routes indicated on 5th Army Area Map showing Traffic Circuits; Overland Tracks to be used if the state of the ground and weather permit.

Details for the move of the 84th Field Company R.E. will be issued later.

H. Ellis Hill
for Capt R.E.
Lieutenant-Colonel
C.R.E., 20th Division.

4th August 1917.

Copies to:-
No. 1. C.R.E., 20th Divn. ✓
2. 83rd Fld.Coy., R.E.
3. 84th Fld.Coy., R.E.
4. 96th Fld.Coy., R.E.
5. G. 20th Divn.
6. Q. 20th Divn.
7. S.S.O. 20th Divn.
8. C.R.E., 38th Divn.
9. C.E., XIV Corps.
10. 20th Divl. Signals.
11. 11th D.L.I.(Pioneers).

SECRET.   Copy No. 1   A.A.55.

C.R.E 20th (LIGHT) DIVISION OPERATION ORDER NO. 29.

Reference attached notes.

1. 84th Field Co., R.E. will take over the right sector dump from 124th Field Co., R.E. and 96th Field Co., R.E. will take over left sector dump from 151st Field Co., R.E. on 6th inst., and make their own arrangements for staffing the dump.

   Transport will be delivering material on that date and unloading parties will be required.

2. 83rd Field Co., R.E. will detail an N.C.O. to report to R.S.M. at ONDANK Dump at 9 a.m. on 6th instant.

   Each Field Company will detail 3 Sappers to report to R.S.M. at same place and time.

   11th D.L.I. will detail 12 pioneers to report to R.S.M. at same place and time.

   These men will be rationed by C.R.E., 20th Division from 7th inclusive and will be accommodated at the dump.

3. R.S.M. GREEN will be in charge of the Divisional Dump at ONDANK and will report on 5th instant to Officer i/c 38th Divisional Dump, which this Division takes over on 6th instant at 11.0 a.m., to get full particulars of the working of the dump. He will send in stock lists to Adjutant R.E. each evening by 6.0 p.m. made up to 4.0 p.m.

4. Sergt: JORDAN will be in charge of the move of H.Q., R.E. detachment and will move off at 9.0 a.m. on 6th.

   Sapper Pemberton will report to Adjutant R.E., 38th Division at DRAGON Camp at 9.0 a.m. on 6th.

5. H.Q., R.E. will close at PROVEN at 9.0 a.m. on 6th inst. and open at DRAGON Camp at the same time.

4th August, 1917.

Captain R.E.,
for C.R.E., 20th Division.

Copy No. 1 C.R.E., 20th Division.
       2 83rd Field Co., R.E.
       3 84th Field Co., R.E.
       4 96th Field Co., R.E.
       5 O.C. 11th D.L.I. (Pioneers).
       6 "Q", 20th Division.
       7 C.R.E., 38th Division.
       8 R.S.M., 20th Division.

R.E. MATERIAL NOTES.

Divisional Dump.   ONDANK, A.5.c.7.3. This is also the Corps Dump, but a portion is reserved for the Division.

Brigade Dump.   AUSTERLITZ to MARENGO Area under charge of 84th Field Co. for right section.
BELMONT to Bridge 6.W Area under charge of 96th Field Co. for left section.

Personnel - ONDANK Dump.   R.S.M., Corporal (83rd Field Co.,R.E.).
3 Sappers from each Company.
4 Pioneers from each Company of 3 Companies 11th D.L.I.
1 Officer & 35 Infantry (Divisional Employment Co.) are accommodated at dump and rationed by C.R.E.
1 Officer and 50 O.R. with haversack rations report daily at 8.0 a.m. and work till 5 p.m.

Transport.   8 lorries report daily at 6.0 a.m., 8 lorries report daily at 8.0 a.m. and make three trips to CANAL Bank.
20 G.S. Wagons report daily at 4.30 a.m. and make one trip to CANAL Bank.
Above are all arranged through "Q" starting on 7th instant.
10 additional G.H.Q. lorries have been arranged occasionally for carrying infantry.
Field Company transport feed forward from CANAL Bank.
11th D.L.I. G.S. wagons draw their own material from ONDANK Dump.

Indents.   Field Companies will indent on Adjutant R.E. by 6 p.m. daily for the material they require on the following day to fill their dump. If additional transport is required Adjutant R.E. must be advised by 12 noon.
All indents on ONDANK Dump must have Adjutant R.E's authority.
Field Companies will make their own regulations for issuing from the Brigade Dumps.

4th August, 1917.

Captain R.E.,
Adjutant R.E., 20th Division.

SECRET.
****

Copy No. ___1___

OPERATION ORDER No. 30
by
C. R. E., 20th DIVISION.

14th August, 1917.

1. The 20th Division will capture and consolidate the enemy's system of trenches shewn on attached tracing on a date and at an hour to be notified later.

2. The attack will be made in three bounds:-

First Bound. - to the BLUE LINE, on which there will be a pause of 20 minutes.

Second Bound.- To the GREEN LINE on which there will be a pause of one hour.

Third Bound. - To the RED LINE.

3. The Division will attack with the 60th Infantry Brigade on the right and the 61st Infantry Brigade on the left, the 59th Infantry Brigade will be in reserve about the canal.
The Divisional boundary and the inter-brigade boundary is shown on attached tracing.

4. B.Gs.C. 60th and 61st Infantry Brigades will assume command of the Right and Left Sub-sectors of the Divisional Front respectively at 10.0 a.m. on August 15th by which hour their Head Quarters will be established as follows:-

60th Infantry Brigade.

    Adv. Hd.Qrs.   STRAY FARM (C.3.c.2.7.)
    Rear Hd.Qrs. Huddersfield Road Dugouts (C.13.c.30.15.)

61st Infantry Brigade.

    Adv. Hd.Qrs.   GDE. BARRIER HOUSE (C.2.b.00.55.)
    Rear Hd.Qrs. FUSILIER HOUSE (C.13.c.10.20)

59th Infantry Brigade HeadQuarters will be at C.19.c.50.05.

5. Field Companies R.E. less transport will be concentrated by 10.0 a.m. August 15th at their present quarters as follows:-

    83rd Field Co., R.E.   C.19.c.3.3.
    84th Field Co., R.E.   C.19.c.2.6.
    96th Field Co., R.E.   B.21.d.3.7.

6. (a). Three sections of the 83rd Field Co., R.E. will construct Strong Points at U.29.a.90.20; U.28.b.85.40; and U.29.a.97.90. and will be under the orders of the G.O.C., 60th Brigade.
The fourth section will construct two road bridges for horse transport between road bridge at U.28.c.85.65 inclusive and Right Divisional Boundary at U.28.d.40.20. The O.C. the Company will have the site reconnoitred and the positions for the bridges marked out as soon as the situation permits, and report to C.R.E. by wire as soon as this has been done.

(b) Three sections of the 84th Field Co., R.E. will construct Strong Points at U.28.b.25.60; U.23.c.55.60; and 46th Kilo stone on Railway at U.22.b.70.15; and will be under the orders of the G.O.C. 61st Infantry Brigade.
The fourth section will construct two road bridges for horse transport between the Railway at U.27.b.95.60 and

- 2 -

destroyed road bridge at U.28.c.85.65 (inclusive). The O.C. the Company will have the site reconnoitred and the positions for the bridges marked out as soon as the situation permits and report to C.R.E. by wire as soon as this has been done.

(c) The 96th Field Co., R.E. will be in reserve and will have two sections ready to carry forward the light railway forward from the neighbourhood of JOLIE FARM (C.9.a.2.8.) in the direction of THE INGS (C.4.a.2.9.) and two sections ready to repair the PILCKEM - IRON CROSS Road Eastward from C.2.b.9.3.

Os.C. 83rd and 84th Field Cos., R.E. will arrange to have taped out "jumping off" lines as required by the G.O.C. Brigades concerned.

7. The 83rd and 84th Field Companies R.E. will remain in readiness at their quarters in the Canal Bank from ZERO onwards.
The three sections of the 83rd and 84th Field Cos. detailed for work on strong points will receive orders to move from B.Gs.C. Infantry Brigades concerned.
The 96th Field Co., R.E. will remain in their quarters at B.21.d.30.70. ready to move at 15 minutes notice two hours after ZERO.

8. Regimental Aid Posts will be established at
(1) IRON POST C.3.a.2.5.
(2) CORNER HOUSE C.2.c.3.7.
and a Forward Advanced Dressing Station at C.8.a.8.3.

9. Dumps of R.E. material have been formed as follows:-
Advanced Dumps at C.3.b.1.9. and U.27.d.45.30.
Reserve Divisional Dump at C.8.a.8.1.
Main Divisional Dump at B.18.d.8.3.

10. Field Companies will detail a cyclist orderly to report to C.R.E. Advanced Headquarters at ELVERDINGHE CHATEAU one hour after ZERO.

11. H.Q., R.E. will open at ELVERDINGHE CHATEAU at 12 noon on 15th August.

12. A C K N O W L E D G E.

Lt.Col., R.E.,
C. R. E., 20th Division.

Copy No. 1 C.R.E.
2 83rd Field Co., R.E. (with tracing)
3 84th Field Co., R.E. ("   ")
4 96th Field Co., R.E. ("   ")
5 "G", 20th Division.
6 "Q" 20th Division.
7. 59th Infantry Brigade.
8 60th Infantry Brigade.
9 61st Infantry Brigade.
10. Chief Engineer, XIV Corps.

Vol 27

War Diary
C.R.E.
20th Divisional
Engineers. Sep. 1917.

WAR DIARY — 20th Divisional R.E.   Army Form C. 2118.

INTELLIGENCE SUMMARY
(Erase heading not required.)

Place	Date	Hour	Summary of Events and Information	Remarks and references to Appendices
	SEPTEMBER 1917.		Reference Maps. 19, 20, 27, 28.	
PROVEN	1		HQRE with Div HQ at PROVEN 27/F7 d.6.9. 83rd Fd Cy RE billeted at 28/B10d. working on forward roads under CE XIV Corps. 83rd Fd Cy RE billeted at 27/2.14.C. erecting NISSEN huts for new Divisional HQ. 96th Fd Cy RE billeted at 27/F.10.a.6.2. training and making frames.	
	7		83rd Cy returned to CROMBEKE area 19/X.29.C.2.1. Front. 83rd and O 7 Bgs relieved the 124th and 123rd Fd Cys of 30th Division on the right sector of the XIVth Corps front with billets at 27/F at 28/B.24 & 26. transferred 28/B.21.d.7.	
	10		84 & at 28/C.19.C.0.7. transferred at 28/B.23.a.3.4. 20th Division relieved the 30th Division on H. Lancemark with right sector of XIV Corps front with HQ including HQRE at WELSH FARM. 28/B.14.C. 96 Fd Cy relieved 151st Cy with billets including transport at B.23 central. 83rd Cy working on tramway 21.10. defence line through Lancemark. 96th Cy on Kenilworth tracks.	
ELVERDINGHE PILCHEM and LANCEMARK	11		RE dumps at ONDANK 28/H.5.C.2.3. BAND at 28/B.10d.1.1. Fd Cy Hdqs BROAD ST at 28/C.R.2.a.2.4. Fd Cy Eqpt Dy. S.A. Tunnel dump. Battle dumps were formed by 83 Fd Cy at 90th Rt.U.22.75 and U.19.a.5.9. Fred 20 material was also delivered in front of STEEN BEKE by T.Cy.	

WAR DIARY or INTELLIGENCE SUMMARY

Army Form C. 2118.

Place	Date	Hour	Summary of Events and Information	Remarks and references to Appendices
SEPTEMBER	19		Rest Coy reorg.	
	20	20.00	Enemy arty active on right attacks at dawn at 5.40 a.m. Enemy not wholly successful at first but general factor after 2 nd attack 8.15 & 9.0 a.m. enemy engaged in strong bands often heard, orders to go forward. Kirg given by B.G.C. D and SY Brig respectively	Paras. Appx. Attacks
	21	8.30	8.30 Coy working on tramway on + duckboard track on right arm. 96 Coy on duckboard track on left.	
	22		Four sections of 96 Coy employed working on Derwent Tank on canal bank. Remaining two on tramway, 2 sections out on salvage in B.20. All remaining two on duckboard track right foundations. 28 Coy 2 section in Derwent Wood in 8.20. one remaining two on duckboard track on LEFT.	
	27		83 Coy returned by 4.00 Pte Gy, reed to camp at 19/K29 C.2.1.	
	28		96 Coy relieved by 328 Pte Gy, reed to camp at 27/F.10.9.1.2	
	29		20. Derwent relieved by 6 Pt reed to position at U.9, military 1905 at 27/F 24/69	
	30		28 Coy relieved by 312 Pte Gy, march to 27/E 17d. 2.51	
			Coy resting Honors. 2/Lt Eckersman R.E. M.C., Pte P.B. answer MC. B. HILLS hgt C Thompson R B.61020 Pte A Baker O.30 Cy answer MM. Sapper G W BANHAM and JS PRILS. 20 Pt Pt Cy answer MM.	

Army Form C. 2118.

WAR DIARY
or
INTELLIGENCE SUMMARY.
(Erase heading not required.)

Place	Date	Hour	Summary of Events and Information	Remarks and references to Appendices
	SEPTEMBER 1917		There were no R.E. casualties on 20th, the day of attack, this being to the Flash Corps doing their consolidation after dark. Casualties for the month: 2 Officers wounded, 1 wounded at duty. 9 O.Rs. killed, 43 wounded, 9 wounded (gas) & wounded at duty.	
			H. Ellis-Hill Capt RE for CRE 20th Div.	

SECRET.

C.R.E., 20th Divn: No.R.A.67.

OPERATION ORDER NO. 36
by
C.R.E., 20th DIVISION.

17th September, 1917.

Reference BROEMBEEK 1/10,000, Edition 2 and LANGEMARK 1/10,000 Edition 2.

1. On a day and at an hour to be communicated later, the XIV Corps, in conjunction with other formations to the South, are continuing the attack on the enemy's positions.
   The XIV Corps attack is being carried out by the 20th Division. The attack will commence simultaneously with that of the XVIII Corps on the right.

2. The 51st Division (XVIII Corps) is on our right; the Guards Division is on our left and does not alter its position.

3. The 20th Division attack will be carried out by two Infantry Brigades, the 60th Infantry Brigade on the right and the 59th Infantry Brigade on the left.

4. The following are shown on the BROEMBEEK 1/10,000 Edition 2 map:-
   (a) The forming up line for the attack - BLACK LINE.
   (b) First objective   - RED DOTTED LINE.
   (c) Second objective   - GREEN LINE.
   (d) Divisional and Inter-Brigade Boundaries.
   (e) Strong points to be made.

5. Head Quarters at Zero will be located as follows:-

   20th Division   WELSH FARM (B.14.c.50.40.)
   59th Infantry Brigade   Adv. ADELPHI C.3.b.17.10.
                            Rear B.23.c.50.80.
   60th Infantry Brigade   Adv. STRAY FARM C.13.c.15.70.
                            Rear HUDDERSFIELD ROAD Dugouts.
   61st Infantry Brigade   FUSILIER HOUSE.

6. The following lines will be consolidated, and in case of counter-attack they will be lines of resistance:-
   (a) GREEN LINE,
   (b) RED DOTTED LINE,
   (c) LANGEMARK Defences.

7. The tasks allotted to Field Companies R.E. are:-
   (a) 83rd Field Company R.E. (with 60th Infantry Brigade)
       One section to each of the strong points at U.24.c.44.43: LOUIS FARM, BLUE HOUSE, U.24.a.75.50.

   (b) 96th Field Company R.E. (with 59th Infantry Brigade)
       One section to each of the strong points at U.23.b.75.53: U.23.b.50.80 (CHINESE HOUSE) U.17.c.87.18: U.17.d.95.00.

   (c) 84th Field Company R.E. will be in Reserve on the Canal Bank and will be prepared to repair and carry forward the duckboards tracks in the Divisional Area.

   The construction of the above strong points will be carried out after dark. Reconnaissance of the sites for the strong points and the setting out of the work should be done before dark.
   The 83rd and 96th Field Companies R.E. will come under orders of B.G's.C. concerned as regards operations on X/Y night. These Companies will arrange direct with B.G's.C. concerned for working parties required for the construction of strong points.
   One Company of the 11th Durham L.I. has been detailed to each of the 59th and 60th Infantry Brigades to assist in the construction of the strong points, the work being supervised by the O.C. Section

/ of the

SECRET.

of the Field Company allotted for the work on strong points.

8. The 83rd and 96th Field Companies R.E. will detail a Liaison Officer for the 60th and 59th Infantry Brigades respectively.

9. Regimental Aid Posts will be at:-

    LANGEMARK   U.29.a.4.9.
    AU BON GITE   U.28.d.2.9.
    CEMENT HOUSE   U.28.c.1.5.
    CORK HOUSE   C.3.a.2.5.

[signature] Capt. R.E.
for
Lt.Col., R.E.
C.R.E., 20th Division.

Copy No.1   C.R.E.
       2   83rd Field Co., R.E.
       3   84th Field Co., R.E.
       4   96th Field Co., R.E.
       5   "G", 20th Division.
       6   "Q", 20th Division.
       7   11th Durham L.I.
       8   B.G.C., 59th Inf. Brigade.
       9   B.G.C., 60th Inf. Brigade.
     10   B.G.C., 61st Inf. Brigade.
     11   20th Divisional Signals.
     12   O.C.183rd Tunnelling Co., R.E.

WO RE 20 P
Vol 28

War Diary

of

20th Divisional Engineers

for month of

October 1917

SECRET.

WAR DIARY 20TH DIVISIONAL R.E.
INTELLIGENCE SUMMARY.
Army Form C. 2118.

(Erase heading not required.)

Place	Date	Hour	Summary of Events and Information	Remarks and references to Appendices
OCTOBER 1917			Reference Maps 27.57c.	
PROVEN	1		HQ RE with Div HQ at PROVEN. 20 Coys entrained for BARAUME from PROVEN.	Sket 27
	2		HQ moved to HAPLINCOURT. Coys arrived at BARAUME. 83rd Coy marched to	" 57c
			BARASTRE, 84th Cy, to YTRES, 96th Cy, to BEAULENCOURT.	
PERONNE	3		HQ moved to PERONNE. 83rd and 84th Cys resting. 96th working on horse	
			standings N24c9.2.	
	4		83rd Cy, marched to SOREL, 84th to HAUT ALLAINES (D.C.) 96th Cy.	
			Continued work on horse standings at N24c9.2.	
	5		83rd Cy marched to billets as follows: 2 Sections Q24.c.2.6, 2 Sections and	"57c
			HQ Q34 and took over work in the line from 231st F.C.y. RE (41st Div) 84th Cy training 96th	
			worked on horse lines at SUZANNE, LE TRANSLOY and Dugout huts.	
	6		83rd Cy, carried on with filling road, maintenance of tramway new gun hut stores, Soft	
			Kitchens and drying room, underground tunnel room in BEETROOT Cp. near BEAUCAMP.	
			hutting in back areas. 96th Cy, moved to W13c	
	7		Two Sections 96th moved to N969.4 (HQ.) and two to Q36d 6.9. Took over from	
			229th F.Cy. 40th Div.	
	8		84th F.Cy and attached infantry marched to SOREL-LE-GRAND. 96th Cy.	

SECRET 20TH DIVISIONAL R.E. Army Form C. 2118.

WAR DIARY
or
INTELLIGENCE SUMMARY.
(Erase heading not required.)

Instructions regarding War Diaries and Intelligence Summaries are contained in F. S. Regs., Part II. and the Staff Manual respectively. Title pages will be prepared in manuscript.

Place	Date	Hour	Summary of Events and Information	Remarks and references to Appendices
OCTOBER 1917				
PERONNE	8		Started work on drawing the front line and RILEY AVE, erecting ADRIAN hut in HEUDECOURT. Shut ST.	
			and Jumping station at GOTHELIEU and GOUZEACOURT.	
	9		84th F.Co. moved to HEUDECOURT and relieved 224th F.Co. (40th Div.), its position	
SOREL-LE-GRAND	10		Spent wk forward billets at VILLERS GUSLAIN	
			H.Q. and K. SOREL-LE-GRAND and took over from 40th Div. (lbh.p.)84th. F. began wk on	
			deep dugouts, M.G. emplacements, trench improvements and huts and horse lines	
	11		in back area. 96th Co drawing and improving front line, GOLF AVE and SYMES AVE	
			Deep dugout starts at R.20 & 2.4th.	
	12		96th Co. working on dugouts R.20.C.2.4th and R.20 d.5.2.K., 2" water main at	
			GOTHELIEU — 35 yds. trench dug 72 ft. main laid	
	13		83rd Co. working on trench maintenance, gun pit stores, Coy kitchens, digging	
			reserve lines near Best Trestles. Continues hutting in back area. 84th Co. on deep dugouts,	
			M.G. emplacements, trench maintenance, hutting. Brigade horse lines reserve Battle Camps, 96th	
	14		making preparation for G.O.C.'s horse at SOREL.	
			96th Co. erected ADRIAN hut in DEVOY Late ROAD.	
	15		96th Co. started foundation for G.O.C.'s horse. Three R.E. teams for HESSERHEIG, DEVOY 2d.	

SECRET

WAR DIARY
or
INTELLIGENCE SUMMARY.

20TH DIVISIONAL R.E. Army Form C. 2118.

Place	Date	Hour	Summary of Events and Information	Remarks and references to Appendices
OCTOBER 1917				
SOREL-LE-GRAND	17		H.Q. and 1 Section 83rd Field Coy moved to found billets in TRESCAULT ROAD.	Sheet 57c
	18		Two Sections 83rd Coy working in huts, repairing and erecting shelters in huts. One Section on wire party. 62 Section making accommodation in TRESCAULT ROAD. 96th Coy draining and erecting SYMES AVE and front line - expanded metal and iron pickets. 100th Coy halts at GOUZEAUCOURT.	
	19		96th Coy, bricklaying GOC's home	
	20		96th Coy cleared 150 yds POPE AVE.	
	21		100 yds POPE AVE cleared	
	22		Lt. R.M.F. HUDDART, 96th F.Coy appointed adj. Capt. VII Corps took over from III Corps.	
	24		a/Capt. R.M.F. HUDDART, 96th F.Coy transferred to 83rd F.Coy. Capt E.B HUGH-JONES 83rd Field Coy transferred to 96th F Coy.	
	25		84th Coy working on deep dugouts, M.G. emplacements and tunnel maintenance and huts in back area. 96th Coy making new horse lines HEUDICOURT.	
	26		83rd Coy mainly employed in trenches, in revetting and putting in small light shelters behind trenches found trench dug with battery 9.4.1 about 1 Kilo well. Enemy before and found new 12" blew found well successfully hidden direct hit from S-Q hill.	

SECRET

WAR DIARY 20TH DIVISIONAL R.E.
INTELLIGENCE SUMMARY
Army Form C. 2118
(Erase heading not required.)

Instructions regarding War Diaries and Intelligence Summaries are contained in F. S. Regs., Part II. and the Staff Manual respectively. Title pages will be prepared in manuscript.

Place	Date	Hour	Summary of Events and Information	Remarks and references to Appendices
OCTOBER 1917	26		96th Fd. Cy. starts new communication trench between NEWPORT TRENCH and front line	57 C
	27		96th Fd. Cy. completes nof of GOC's horse. hand task on new communication trench completed. a/Capt. (temp. Lt.) H.N. COALES, M.C., R.E. assumes duties of Adjutant. Lt. H.E. HILL, M.C., R.E., temporarily attached to 94th Fd Cy.	
	28		96th Fd. Cy. completes new communication trench from NEWPORT TRENCH & front line	
	29		96th Fd. Cy. made bombing stop in JOM Cop. hew support line starts from RILEY & FOSTER AVE. III Corps task over from VIII Corps. II Cpl. STOKES, G., 83rd Fd Cy, R.E. awarded military medal. III Corps Defence Scheme: FIMS. V12 C. 'TYKE', W 3 d (R.S.M., 39 infantry (small supporters) 4 points start) and 12 sappers) 'BOX', W17 C 22 (14th Bg, troops) Divisional bombs.	
			Casualties for month - NIL	

H.E. Coales
Capt R.E.
for C.R.E. 20th Division

No RG 120
Vol 29

20th Division - Engineers

War Diary

November 1917

Army Form C. 2118.

WAR DIARY
or
INTELLIGENCE SUMMARY.
(Erase heading not required.)

20TH DIVISIONAL R.E.

Place	Date	Hour	Summary of Events and Information	Remarks and references to Appendices
	NOVEMBER 1917			
SOREL	14		96th Coy. working at roads and tracks to fill gaps near model at SOREL	Sketch 77c
	15		HISSETT hits hind ends at M9 d 7.3 & Pile Hep. Rest of Coy. filled in shell holes
	16		91st Coy. making country track from Wood to MST
	17		1 section 83rd Coy. employed making track for Q.F. 6 in. and work to lines
			remainder of section headed on work to G.F. 6in. and work to lines at HEUDECOURT
	18		96th Coy. erecting screens on CORPS ROAD.
	19		83rd Coy. put 13 wooden bridge across trench, 24th Coy. 23 bridges
HEUDECOURT	20		Moved forward to advanced H.Q. near HEUDECOURT 6am and detraments at 3 p.m. to H.Q. at VILLERS PLOUICH. Attack on HINDENBURG line opened not ministure took Posn 83rd Coy. employed as follows. 1 section to VILLERS PLOUICH and worked on making tanks, cleaning wire, bridges
VILLERS PLOUICH			& VILLERS PLOUICH. 1 section in the attack with 60th Bde. Rode. 3 sections mines to tanks and reconnaissance for water supply. 84th Coy. moved to VILLERS PLOUICH not tonight. 1 section in attack with 61st Inf. Bde. and made tow King fords M and N5. 9 Lt VICKERIE 96th Coy. moved to VILLERS PLOUICH. 1 section in attack with Better but demolish bridge at G35d 3.4 and M5e58

No RG 20P
Vol 29

November 1917

War Diary

50th Divisional Engineer

SECRET

Army Form C. 2118.

Instructions regarding War Diaries and Intelligence Summaries are contained in F.S. Regs., Part II. and the Staff Manual respectively. Title pages will be prepared in manuscript.

WAR DIARY
or
INTELLIGENCE SUMMARY.
(Erase heading not required.)

20TH DIVISIONAL RE

Place	Date	Hour	Summary of Events and Information	Remarks and references to Appendices
NOVEMBER 1917				
SOREL	1		HQ RE with Divn at SOREL-LE-GRAND. 83rd Field Coy HQ at GOUZEAUCOURT —	Sheet 57c
			The scouts Road 84th Field Coy at HEUDECOURT. 96th Field Coy now HEUDECOURT	
			with forward parties. 83rd Coy working with 8th Brigade in line, also at Brigade	
			Camp Huts, supply OPs, trench mortar emplacements and dugouts. 1 Officer	
			and 2 NCOs running British School for cattle. 84th Coy working on huts	
			in back area round HEUDECOURT. Re-siting in line in front of MULLEZ	
			GUISLORT on MG emplacements, water supply and trench maintenance. 96th	
			Coy erecting huts & section on GOC's quarters, 1 section Q.C. horse lines and 2	
			sections with forward on trench maintenance.	
	2		95th Coy completed hutment shop & 10M tank.	
	3		96th Coy commenced work on a well near SOREL. Coy now engaged	
			hutting 12th officers quarters. GOC's hutment completely kept	
			light shaft up to 30 yards.	
	4		GOC's quarters at HEUDECOURT completed. 2 latrines 95 Coy made road and	
			gun pits at HEUDECOURT, filling completed in dugs and Red & S.	
			Upon trench maintenance and improvements	

WAR DIARY
INTELLIGENCE SUMMARY

Army Form C. 2118.
20th Divisional R.E.

Place	Date	Hour	Summary of Events and Information	Remarks and references to Appendices
SOREL	NOVEMBER 1917			Sheet 57c
SOREL	5		1 section 96th Coy moved to SOREL for work on road from GOUZEAUCOURT	
	6		83rd Coy employed in making accommodation for mountain in stables. 96th Coy under orders made sure of NEW stables and swan nets in GOUZEAUCOURT	
	7		83rd Coy on trestling. Report state camp at HEUDECOURT also huttings at RAILWOOD Camp and from enemy station in FINS-NUBLU road. 84th Coy started on accommodation for Batallion at H.Q. This rendered completely camp intel / accommodation at a height of 5'6" for the guard and found it to be unsuitable for the use	
	8		96th Coy continued work on road in GOUZEAUCOURT, cleaning out support trench and making night paths for fatigues across the state system	
	9		83rd Coy continued work on pretty steel shelters	
	10		96th Coy making fresh dugout for Signals	
	11		96th Coy work on road tunnel carried on board tramway made	
	12			
	13		96th Coy stables constructed for Signals dugouts in ARGYLE LANE and RILEY Ave.	

Army Form C. 2118.

WAR DIARY
or
INTELLIGENCE SUMMARY.
(Erase heading not required.)

20TH DIVISIONAL R.E.

Place	Date	Hour	Summary of Events and Information	Remarks and references to Appendices
NOVEMBER 1917				Sheet 57c
SOREL	14		96th Fy. getting out roads and standing to fill shell holes at SOREL	
	15		MISSERY huts hut duties at my d.7.3 & Bde HQ. Rest at SOREL finish	
	16		91st Fy. making country track from N16d & N15b	
	17		1 Section 93rd Fy. emptying mining trucks for Tank in fines area. Remainder of Section handed over work to 65th Fy. and moved to stores at HEUDECOURT	
	18		96 Fy. erecting screens on CORBIE ROAD	
	19		83rd Fy. put 13 width bridge over canal, 64th Fy. 23 width bridge and bridgework. Moved fwd to advanced HQ near HEUDECOURT 6 am. Attack on HINDENBURG line started with machines of Tank Bde. 93rd Fy. empty'g & filling in. 3 section moved	
HEUDECOURT	20		83rd Fy. 1 section in the attack with 60th & 61st Bde.	
VILLERS PLOUICH			to VILLERS PLOUICH and acted on advanced stores, clearing wire, bridges, and reconnaissance etc into supply. 84th Fy. 2 sections to VILLERS PLOUICH not employed on attack, 1 section in attack with 61st Inf Bde and made the King from N and NE of LA VACQUERIE. 91st Fy. through to VILLERS PLOUICH — bridges in attack with 59th Bde at G33d.3. and MSc5.A	

Army Form C. 2118.

WAR DIARY
or
INTELLIGENCE SUMMARY.
(Erase heading not required.)

20TH DIVISIONAL R.E.

Instructions regarding War Diaries and Intelligence Summaries are contained in F. S. Regs., Part II. and the Staff Manual respectively. Title pages will be prepared in manuscript.

Place	Date	Hour	Summary of Events and Information	Remarks and references to Appendices
VILLERS PLOUICH	NOVEMBER 1917			
	20		This could not be accepted as the infantry were not in possession of the bridge heads and were not put not sufficient fields to secure them.	
	21		83rd Cy making a track and note supply. 84th Cy clearing another road from LA VACQUERIE to MASNIÈRES. Meyrick & Lucas bridge M.29.b. 84th Coy wired main line of resistance N.E. of LATEAU wood. Another attempt to demolish bridge at M.5C.2.2 fails for some reason to explode.	
	22		83rd Coy wiring between G33a.7.6 and G33a.9.0. 96th Cy wiring G33c.6.0.	
	23		-M3c.8.0.-M3c.6.0. 83rd Coy dugout near main road G4t.b.6. Bde. H.Q. Road sloping from main rd at the crossroads G32d.6.0 in appearance front 84th and 96th wiring.	
	24		83rd Cy putting shelters in sunken roads and carrying supplements all day H.Q. 2 sector. 84th Cy road from to dugouts in HINDENBURG line.	
	25		96th Cy improving accommodation in SURREY RIDGE.	
	26			
	27		both continue on wiring and work in the R. centre.	
	28		Light actions between M3a.l.5. and G33b.2.8.	

1577 Wt. W10791/1773 500,000 1/15 D. D. & L. A.D.S.S./Forms/C. 2118.

Army Form C. 2118.

WAR DIARY
or
INTELLIGENCE SUMMARY.
(Erase heading not required.)

20TH DIVISIONAL R.E.

Place	Date	Hour	Summary of Events and Information	Remarks and references to Appendices
NOVEMBER 1917				
VILLERS PLOUICH	29		Reconnaissance made of dug-outs and entrance to R.E.	
	30		Summer made for return on 29th Nov. and sgt. 83rd fields. 83rd Co. lost 1 officer and 12 O.R. wounded and the senior N.C.O. Red Cap. manned the trenches.	H. A. Clerke Capt. R.E. for CRE 20th Division

Vol 30

War Diary

of

20th Divisional Engineers

for

December 1917.

WAR DIARY of INTELLIGENCE SUMMARY

20TH DIVISIONAL R.E.

Army Form C. 2118.

Place	Date	Hour	Summary of Events and Information	Remarks and references to Appendices
B DUGOUT Q 24 C	DECEMBER 1/12/17	30/17	Div. HQ. moved from VILLERS PLOUICH to 'B' Dugout near QUEENS CROSS. Div Res Coys were still standed in support and being taken on fatigues. 83rd Coy recovering her Fusilier and Dumrevert trenches. The 84th Res Coy in the 47th Bde of R.E. returned to Bde at GREEN at NIGHT. The 96th Coy. in trench the line with the 7th Batt. ROYAL Etc. to first knoll by HINDENBURG Line had apparently withdrawn to hill a trench enclosed FIFTEEN RAVINES 96th Coy taking RILEY AVE. and a portion of the front line.	Sheet 57 c
	2		84th & and 96th Coys. held the line	
SOREL-LE-GRAND	3		HQ RE moved to SOREL-LE-GRAND at about 9 P.M. 84th Coy moved to VILLERS at midnight and 96th Coy to SOREL.	
BAIZIEUX	4		Div. HQ moved to BAIZIEUX. 83rd Coy embushed party marching to YPRES, went by train to BUIRE; marched to billets nr VARENNES. 84th Coy – to billets to Dummanie – by bus to VILLE-SOUS-CORBIE, all companies marched to MEAULTE. 83rd Coy Tanglet her transport to ORVILLE	AMIENS PINCH
	5		Southampton 84th and 96th Coys. tanglet together to ORVILLE	
	6		HQ RE moved with Div Hd to HOCQUELIERS, train transport from Tr. Cl. PUCHEVILLERS	

WAR DIARY or INTELLIGENCE SUMMARY

Army Form C. 2118.

20TH DIVISIONAL R.E.

Place	Date	Hour	Summary of Events and Information	Remarks and references to Appendices
DECEMBER 1917				
HOCQUELIERS	6		to X Corps. Second Army. 83rd Cy with party of transport marched to AVELUY. went to kin to HESDIN and readers from there to MARGIVAL transport marched to FILLIEVRES. 84th Cy to station to HESDIN, the marched to CREQUY. transport marched to BOUBERS. 96th Cy to above to HESDIN, then marched ST DEVREUX. transport marched to AUBROMETZ, all transport with 60 ZD Coy Trans T. 14	CALAIS Road 13 ABBEVILLE Road 14
	7		and 59th Bdes transport, respectively. 83rd Cy marched to GOEUFFY and no remained to transport 84th Cy Trans marched to HEMOVILLE. transport 96 Cy to transport marched to HEMOVILLE. transport 84th Cy arrived ST DEVREUX.	
	8		to PLUMPTSON transport 84 Cy moved HEMOVILLE.	
	9		Conference Knowl.	
	10		96 Cy to reconnaissance marched to HUMBERT. moved there by bus to	
	11		RECONNAISSANCE transport marched to THIEMBRONNE.	
BLARINGHEM	12		Div HQ moved to BLARINGHEM and transferred to IX Corps Second Army. 84 Cy moved by bus into BLARINGHEM area transport moved to THIEMBRONNE.	HAZEBROUCK 5A
	13		83rd Cy moved to ST CROCQUET. 96 Cy transport moved.	
	14		CRE proceeded on one month leave to UK. Major P. F. STORY, D.S.O.R.E. of 96th Div Cy acting CRE. H.Q. RE moved to ELZENWALLE.	Road 28
ELZENWALLE				

Army Form C. 2118.

WAR DIARY
or
INTELLIGENCE SUMMARY.
(Erase heading not required.)

20TH DIVISIONAL R.E.

Instructions regarding War Diaries and Intelligence Summaries are contained in F. S. Regs., Part II. and the Staff Manual respectively. Title pages will be prepared in manuscript.

Place	Date	Hour	Summary of Events and Information	Remarks and references to Appendices
	DECEMBER 1917			Sheet 28.
ELZENWALLE	15		CRE. 11th A. attended conference at IX Corps reference Army Defence Scheme.	
			Transport 249. S. and to STRAZEELE.	
			84th S. and some pack animals at R.E. Farm. KEMMEL (mud) transport.	
			229th Coy. marches to STRAZEELE	
	16			
	17		83rd S. and transport moved to R.E. Farm	
	18		96th S. transport and camp & moved. Billet improvements in BAILLEULEM area	
	19		83rd S. Field S., 84th S. Field S., XI Bnn. D.L.I. (Pion.) and two infantry	
			battalions (1st 6th K.S.L.I. and 7th K.O.Y.L.I.) subsequently 10 S. and 11th R.B.)	
			employed on camp & up and around Corps line, 3 battns of divisional troops. First into find at first with	
			about 30 ft. and 37th divisional front, first into find at first with	
	31		on the Corps there billets could obtain about 40 yds front completed.	

A. Cole
Capt. R.E.
for CRE 20th Division.

Vol 31

War Diary

of

20th Divisional Engineers

January 1918

SECRET

Army Form C. 2118.

WAR DIARY
or
INTELLIGENCE SUMMARY.
(Erase heading not required.)

20TH DIVISIONAL R.E.

Instructions regarding War Diaries and Intelligence Summaries are contained in F. S. Regs., Part II. and the Staff Manual respectively. Title pages will be prepared in manuscript.

Place	Date	Hour	Summary of Events and Information	Remarks and references to Appendices
	JANUARY 1918.			Sheet 29
ELZENWALLE	4		83rd and 84th Coys. working on Coy Line near (HAZEBROUCK SA) 96th Coy. Training in BLARINGHEM area (HAZEBROUCK SA).	
	5		2 section 84th Coy meet parties for R.E. Recon (Mead 9.2.) at CANADA tunnels (I30 a 5.0).	
	6		84th Coy. moved forward to CANADA Tunnels. Coy Line near 62nd & 2nd section 84th Coy. moved from BLARINGHEM area to VOORMEZEELE Continuing. 96th Coy.	
	7		83rd, 84th Coys. rope to have one work from 30th Bde R.E. 83rd Hd. JACKDAW Rd.	
NESTOUTRE	8		20th Division relieved 30th Division in the MERTIM ROAD Sector. Hd at NESTOUTRE. 83rd Coy working on Tunis tram tracks. Left Bn. H.Q. and MERTIM Road tunnels. 50 attached infantry jus'd sap. G. working on Reserve Line near (double apron) - main line of defence.	
	9		96th Coy working on new Project Reserve Line near H30 c 63 83rd Coy wiring main Line of Resistance. Returning pill boxes. Improvement to OKAP at SMART CHATEAU. 96th Coy. wiring PERTH AVENUE.	
	10		Reserve line wiring being continued. 96th Coy. completes one shelter, E.P. N° 3	
	11		work on PERTH AVENUE continued	
	12		Two belts of double apron wire completed in front of Reserve Line, 61st Inf Bde front. Total length 1800 yds.	

SECRET.

Instructions regarding War Diaries and Intelligence Summaries are contained in F. S. Regs., Part II. and the Staff Manual respectively. Title pages will be prepared in manuscript.

Army Form C. 2118.

WAR DIARY
or
INTELLIGENCE SUMMARY.
(Erase heading not required.)

20TH. DIVISIONAL R.E.

Place	Date	Hour	Summary of Events and Information	Remarks and references to Appendices
	JANUARY 1918.			Sheet 28
WESTOUTRE	13		282 Cy. wiring Brown Line & Rintraw. 84th Cy. working on NO 7 stray Point. 96. Cy. completed 120ft breastwork screen E end of PERTH AVENUE. 75 I.W. A frame and duckboards to NO 3 S.R. quarters. Burying not in use. Bay Cut bomb pit line H30C.	
	14		282 Cy. stakes third belt of wire along Brown line & Rintraw. 50 yd completed. 96 Cy. working at SUBORDINATE POSN. proposed to the Ruxtray M.G. stray Post. C.R.E. retained two have to U.K.	
	15		282 Cy. same work line & Rintraw. 96 Cy. battery, H30 C. Ruxtray not deeper	
	16		MG Coys working M.L.R. 96 Cy. battery, H30 C. Ruxtray not deeper	
	17		I.17.c.3.5. (RITZ DUGOUT) wire continued.	
	18		Relieved by RITZ dug out continued	
	19		84th Cy. working on stray pits NO. 6 & 7.	
	20		96 ½ Cy. wiring SUBURBS LINE, DUMBARTON MSD. Ruxtray SP L 5.	
	21		Camouflage stray front made by concealing of steel pits and covering with road screening. Quite inconspicuous. (952 g) 96 Cy. Burying 185 250 Rounds.	

WAR DIARY

INTELLIGENCE SUMMARY.

20TH DIVISIONAL R.E.

Army Form C. 2118.

Place	Date	Hour	Summary of Events and Information	Remarks and references to Appendices
JANUARY 1918				
NESTOOTRE	22		83rd Coy. inspected the new S.P.'s in M.L.R. Had to be moved partly, in trenches very conspicuous and difficult to camouflage. Wiring of M.L.R. and Retrench line continued.	Sheet 25
	23		Wiring continued. Reinforcing of R.H.P. dugouts. 96th Coy. Wiring POPPY AVE.	
	24		96th Coy. erecting shelter in No.5 S.P. Gap being cut in wire and extra bands fixed – 2 GAP IN WIRE	
	25		No. 7 S.P. at -.26 a 7.9 renumbered No. 2, No. 5 SP. at -.20 at 4T30 No.3. S.P's now numbered right to left.	
	26		Wiring continued.	
	27		83rd Coy. making new huts for Batty and other inspection – one near STRAZELE CARTER and one near DICKEBUSCH; wiring FORESTER CAMP. 96th Coy. working on S.P.'s 1, 2 and 3	
	28		83rd Coy. protecting front of H.Q. of Tunnellers, damaged by rain. 96th Coy. wiring Rhenwick Line, 96th Coy. front tactical entrance to R.E.M. in rear to their battery positions.	
	29		83rd Coy. stables & cook house YMCA hut near FORESTER CAMP 96th Coy. opening up defences of PALESTINE TRENCH	
	30		Wiring continued	
	31		84th Coy. erected STEVENS TRENCH 300 ft. 2st. for all round defence	[signature] Capt. R.E. for LtE 20th Dr [signature] Capt. R.E. for LtE 20th Dr

SECRET
Army Form C. 2118.

WAR DIARY
INTELLIGENCE SUMMARY. H.Q. 20TH DIVISIONAL R.E.

(Erase heading not required.)

Instructions regarding War Diaries and Intelligence Summaries are contained in F.S. Regs., Part II. and the Staff Manual respectively. Title pages will be prepared in manuscript.

VM 32

Place	Date	Hour	Summary of Events and Information	Remarks and references to Appendices
FEBRUARY 1918				
WESTOUTRE	1		83rd F.Coy working on POLDERHOEK sector, 84th F.Coy working on main line of Resistance, MENIN Rd between 96th F.Coy working on Intermediate line from Line of Resistance to rear support line. Rear section of 96th F.Coy working on Tramline between VIJVER HOEK	Sketch 28
	2			
	3		83rd F.Coy continued and erected front & support lines, putting in small light posts. Also erecting Y.M.C.A. hut KRUISSTRAATHOEK	
	4		Coy erecting NISSEN huts in Kampfort line H.30.C	
	5/6/7		Work continued as above	
	8		83rd F.Coy. There are work on left extending over our Battalion front for New Zealand Division. Already supply and meeting Support to Reserve line.	
	9		96th F.Coy. M.A. huts from I.31.a.1.7 to new NISSEN huts around H.30.C.4	
	10		96th F.Coy working on Intermediate line and Main Line of Resistance, GHELUVELT Sector	
			96 F.Coy. In trenches being continued to be called Coy.	
	11/12/13/14		Work in line continued as above	
	15		83rd F.Coy Kampfort moved to STERZEELE	
	16		83rd Coy entrained to EBBINGHEM, then marching to encampment ground by train at STERZEELE	
			84th F.Coy & 96th F.Coy Kampfort marched to STERZEELE	HAZEBROUCK 5.A
BLARINGHEM	17		Div. H.Q. moved to BLARINGHEM. 24th and 96th F.Coy (Pioneers) entrained at DICKEBUSCH the	

SECRET

Army Form C. 2118.

WAR DIARY
of
INTELLIGENCE SUMMARY.

H.Q. 20TH DIVISIONAL R.E.

(Erase heading not required.)

Instructions regarding War Diaries and Intelligence Summaries are contained in F. S. Regs., Part II. and the Staff Manual respectively. Title pages will be prepared in manuscript.

Place	Date	Hour	Summary of Events and Information	Remarks and references to Appendices
BLARINGHEM	17		EBBLINGHEM, marching to HEURINGHEM and RACQUINGHEM respecting. Gms & Transport	Rest HAZEBROUCK 5A
	18 19		Rides Gps. training. Bivouac equipment redrawn from 9 E. Pontoon Park. Preparing to leave. Hostile aircraft Amiel.	
	20		8.30 am & 84 E. Gp. training. 96 E. G. marched to STEENBECQUE and entrained for NESLE (AMIENS)	
	21		83 E. G. marched to STEENBECQUE and entrained for NESLE. 84 E. G. marched to RACQUINGHEM. 96 E. G. arrived at NESLE and marched to CAMPAGNE.	
ERCHEU (XVIII Corps HQ TROOPS)	22		Div. HQ. moved to ERCHEU by rail. 84 E. G. marched to STEENBECQUE and entrained for NESLE. 83 E. and 96 E. Gp. training.	AMIENS 17
	23		84 E. G. arrived at NESLE and marched to TIELANCOURT	
	24 to 28		Gps. training.	

Wh Cook
Capt. R.E.
for CRE 20 E. Division

20th Divisional Engineers

C. R. E.

20th DIVISION.

MARCH 1918

SECRET

WAR DIARY
INTELLIGENCE SUMMARY

HQ. 20TH DIVISIONAL ENGINEERS

Army Form C. 2118.

Place	Date	Hour	Summary of Events and Information	Remarks and references to Appendices
ERCHEU	MARCH 1918 1, 2, 3		With Divisional HQ at ERCHEU. Field Coys. training in the area. 83rd and 84th Corps moved to HQ at SOMMETTE EAUCOURT and CANIZY, respectively, with detailed defensive schemes for work on Rear Zone defences under C.E. XVIII Corps, and eventually C.E. Cavalry Corps. 96th F.C. moved to HQ at CHAULNES for work on sector 'B'.	Sheets AMIENS 17 & ST QUENTIN 14
	4		Reconnaissance of 'green' line - i.e. Rear Zone defences -	
	5-19		Work on Rear Zone defences. There carried the principals of 'support' system at 500 yds interval, with equal numbers of supporting posts 250 yds in rear. Counter attack batteries 500 yds in rear of front outposts. One battalion front had 2000 yds and [?] 16 M.G.s, the whole supply at defence in depth. The latter available were eventually three Subs Coys, 6 F[?] Army Troops, 5 R.E. by 1st Lat. Bde., 3 Coys. of O.L.H. (Royals), 10 Western Labour Coys, & Salvage Bulk. Defences limited from west roughly from ESSOME (between B and C)	
	20	5.30am	To 6.30. Germans attack line more in training, advanced to dominating information that [?] the German attack was imminent, that a letter 'B' and 'C' Coys. on by Majs. HULL, and Reid Quintin R.E. and 5 Field Engineer officers, Cavalry Corps	

SECRET.

Army Form C. 2118.

WAR DIARY
INTELLIGENCE SUMMARY.
(Erase heading not required.)

Instructions regarding War Diaries and Intelligence Summaries are contained in F. S. Regs., Part II. and the Staff Manual respectively. Title pages will be prepared in manuscript.

HQ. 20TH DIVISIONAL ENGINEERS

Place	Date	Hour	Summary of Events and Information	Remarks and references to Appendices
	MARCH 1918.			
ERCHEU	21	5.30 AM.	German offensive opened. Warning order received: "XVIII Corps manning battle stations". Reports R.E. Gp. standing by to move.	Sheet AMIENS 17
		4 PM.	Divisional H.Q. moved to HAM. Zinc Gp. all concentrated at ST. SULPICE, spare transport and bridging wagons at VERLAINES. 61st Div. H.Q. Rd. 84th Coy. reported for work under orders of 61st Div. Rd. attached to 36th Division.	ST. QUENTIN 18
HAM	22		at DURY. 84th Coy. moved to OLLEZY. 2 Section 83rd Coy. reported for work to 61st Div. R.E. at AUBIGNY, 2 Section 96th Coy. to 59th Bde. at VILLERS-ST-CHRISTOPHE digging and wiring trenches.	
		9 PM.	Divisional H.Q. moved to EPPEVILLE. Orders received for demolition of bridges over LA SOMME CANAL. 83rd and 96th Cys. instructed. These were reported to have been previously prepared for demolition by another division, but it was not so found to have been done in many instances, in an unsatisfactory manner and a considerable amount of additional work had to be done on them.	
EPPEVILLE	23	about 5 PM.	Divisional H.Q. moved to NESLE. R.E. Gp. moved all spare transport to CAREPUIS. R.O.Dr. demolished over LA SOMME Canal.	Sheet AMIENS 17

SECRET

Army Form C. 2118.

WAR DIARY
INTELLIGENCE SUMMARY
H.Q. 20TH DIVISIONAL ENGINEERS

(Erase heading not required.)

Instructions regarding War Diaries and Intelligence Summaries are contained in F.S. Regs., Part II. and the Staff Manual respectively. Title pages will be prepared in manuscript.

Place	Date	Hour	Summary of Events and Information	Remarks and references to Appendices
	MARCH 1918.			Sheet AMIENS 17
NESLE	23		Small dumps of tools wire and pickets found outside NESLE, principally to the N.W. on NESLE–BEUVRE line. This being worked by 3 Field Coys. & 61st Div. and Various Corps Troops. Stores not sound. The safety of R.E. Park, CHAULNES, but vital to some firms deliberately acting for No 6 R.E. Park, CHAULNES, but before the enemy were anywhere near it & consequences, for some three days parties not hand had great difficulty in getting stores from the Park owing to the great heat and inaccessibility of many materials. The Park appears to have been abandoned by its staff and the stores presumably are left to the enemy. Bde. light artillery. 83rd and 96th Bde. ordered to report for work to	
	24		83rd Coy. ordered to Bde. to form defensive flank on left ground running N.E. & S.W. on mile E. of HOMBLEUX, started by strengthening from 20th Div. and 1 Coy. from S.M. with 12th K.R.R.C. on left, right flank in the air; holes up several attacks until our left retirement on flank is withdrawn & hole to E.G. troops at 3.45 p.m. 83rd Coy. withdrawn to BILLANCOURT. A later so E. G. was formed by D.A.I. and occupies a line a CUGNY - VILLESEUE road and 7 p.m. with elements of 61st Bde. 96th Coy. supporting line from QUIQUERY & NESLE-ITT.	
NICAISE				
ETHOMVILLERS		2 P.M.	Div. H.Q. moved to RETHONVILLERS.	

SECRET

Army Form C. 2113.

WAR DIARY
INTELLIGENCE SUMMARY.
(Erase heading not required.)

HQ. 20TH DIVISIONAL ENGINEERS

Place	Date	Hour	Summary of Events and Information	Remarks and references to Appendices
MARCH 1918				Sheet Annex "1"
RETHONVILLERS	24		Strength of Shunks found all round B/fort. MESLE Sector. Ref. Bdes. informed. Quantity of Kensims taken over from 61st Div. and returned to Field Engs. 83rd and 96th Coys. less one feature each overnight at BILLANCOURT allergies.	
CAREPUIS	25	3 PM	Div. H.Q. moved to CAREPUIS at 3 PM. 83rd and 96th Coys employed on deft line north CREMERY. Deft. control by Xrm. Corps for 61st Bde. on detour near LIANCOURT.	
ROYE.	-	10 PM	Div. HQ. moved KROYE	
	26		Div HQ and 83rd & 96th Field Coys meet L'ECHELLE. Almost unknown on arrival. Heavy reports. Bde. close behind. 84th F. Cy. meet to MEZIERES, no further details. Attached 61st Bde. Left of Shunk received by Corps for XVIII Corps.	
LE QUESNEL	27		JRE. G.S. appt. bne. of fnts. E. of HANGEST-EN-SANTERRE and LE QUESNEL	
	28		Div HQ and all Field Coys. moved to DOMART-SUR-LUCE. Rec. Coys. appd. new line near DEMUIN - MOREUIL road	
DOMART SUR-LA-LUCE	29		Ditto	
BOVES	30		Div HQ moved to BOVES. Field Coys moved to billets in BOVES. Employed in digging new line. Sech. 7 Barrs DE GENTELLES	Anxd. Captured
	31		Coys in rest at BOVES	For CRE. 20th Division

SECRET Army Form C. 2118.

Instructions regarding War Diaries and Intelligence Summaries are contained in F.S. Regs., Part II. and the Staff Manual respectively. Title pages will be prepared in manuscript.

WAR DIARY
INTELLIGENCE SUMMARY.
(Erase heading not required.)

H.Q. 20TH DIVISIONAL ENGINEERS.

WO 34

Place	Date	Hour	Summary of Events and Information	Remarks and references to Appendices
	APRIL 1918.			
BOVES	1		Division retired in line of 14th Division. Division moved to NAMPS-AU-MONT night 1/2	Sheet AMIENS 7.
NAMPS-AU-MONT	2		Field Coys dug in line W. of GENTELLES, then entrained for AMIENS - ROYE Rd & FRESNOY AU-VAL, 8.30 P.M.	
QUEVAUVILLERS	3		Div. H.Q. moved to QUEVAUVILLERS. Divl. Engs. marched to ST-AUBIN-MONTENOY	
	4-8		Divl. Engs. refitting and training.	
BROCOURT	9		C.R.E. & H.Q. marched with Divl. Engs. to BROCOURT	Sheet DIEPPE 16
HUPPY	10		C.R.E. & Div. H.Q. moved to HUPPY. 83rd Divl Coy marched to BAILLEUL, 94th Coy to LE PLOUY, 96th Coy to BOUTTENCOURT-SUR-GAMACHES. (Sheet DIEPPE 16.)	Sheet ABBEVILLE
GAMACHES	11		Div. H.Q. moved to GAMACHES. 83rd 94th 96th Coys marched to VISME, 84th Coy to OUST-MAREST. 96th Coy to BEAUCHAMPS	
	12		Conference training.	
	13		83rd Coy moved to BEAUCHAMPS	
	14-17		Training. Infantry drill, musketry and Inf'y work. Portion of all Coys half day & half day for PORT REMY	
VILLERS CHATEL	18		Div. H.Q. moved to VILLERS CHATEL by Gr. Divisional portion of Divl. Engs. and part of transport entrained at EU night 18/19 for same area	Sheet LENS 11.
	19		83rd Coy marched from TIMQUES Station to billets at GAUCHIN LEGAL, 24-25.	

SECRET

Army Form C. 2118.

WAR DIARY
or
INTELLIGENCE SUMMARY.
(Erase heading not required.)

HQ 20TH DIVISIONAL ENGINEERS

Instructions regarding War Diaries and Intelligence Summaries are contained in F. S. Regs., Part II. and the Staff Manual respectively. Title pages will be prepared in manuscript.

Place	Date	Hour	Summary of Events and Information	Remarks and references to Appendices
VILLERS CHATEL	APRIL 1918			Pencil LBMS 11
	19		To MARQUAY. 96th S. & GESTREVILLE Field Coys. training.	
	20 & 21		84th Cy. moved with 61st Dy. Bde to CAMBLAIN L'ABBE	
	29			
	30		Lt. V.G. HOLGATE transferred from 83rd Bde, & L 22nd in command of 84th. Field Cy. on from 25/3/18	Attack apell forces in L. Simon

WAR DIARY
of
INTELLIGENCE SUMMARY. H.Q. 20TH DIVISIONAL ENGINEERS
(Erase heading not required.)

Army Form C. 2118.

WC 35

Place	Date	Hour	Summary of Events and Information	Remarks and references to Appendices
	MAY 1918			
VILLERS CHATEL	1		Division training. 83rd Field Cy. at GAUCHIN LEGAL, 84th at CAMBLAIN L'ABBÉ, 96th at Sheet 44B.	
VILLERS-AU-BOIS	2		Division moved to VILLERS-AU-BOIS relieving Lens and Arras Sectors from 4th and 3rd Canadian Division. 83rd Cy. relieved at X17.6.4.2 (SOUCHEZ) relieving 7th Canadian Field Cy, 84th Cy. took over trench at N13.6.7.a and S6.6.4.2 and formed work from 7th Can. Field Cy, 96th Cy. took over camp at ABLAIN-ST-NAZAIRE.	ST NAZAIRE RIVER
	3		83rd Cy. took over work in forward trench and tanks at SCURY (IRISH SUPPORT) from 84th Cy. the latter employed on maintenance of road services in vicinity of SOUCHEZ. Dist depôt and tank maintenance.	
	4		3 platoons 96th Cy. moved to "Gibbs" in LIÉVIN. Existing work in LENS Sector Recce tips. pushed all bridge equipment with No1 Pontoon Park under Army arrangements.	
CHATEAU-DE-LA-HAIE	7		Divisional H.Q. moved to CHATEAU-DE-LA-HAIE. 83rd Cy. later in defny zone wiring and frontal point.	
	9		Divisional defence scheme inaugurated 84th Cy. in front of Divisional Reserve Line and to man ARTHUR'S SEAT. 83rd Cy. to be held in reserve near SOUCHEZ. 84th Cy. manning Hill 63 making artillery tracks, also manning MISSISSIPPI hut at	
	10		camp near SOUCHEZ and presently at ABLAIN-ST-NAZAIRE.	
	11		96th Cy. making a trench mortar and dugout CARENCY-LA-ROME. Parks out and park work.	

SECRET.

Army Form C. 2118.

WAR DIARY
of
INTELLIGENCE SUMMARY.
(Erase heading not required.)

HQ 20TH DIVISIONAL ENGINEERS

Instructions regarding War Diaries and Intelligence Summaries are contained in F. S. Regs., Part II. and the Staff Manual respectively. Title pages will be prepared in manuscript.

Place	Date	Hour	Summary of Events and Information	Remarks and references to Appendices
CHATEAU-DE-LA-HAIE	MAY 1918.			Sheet 44B & ST. NAZAIRE RIVER
	13		83rd Coy. started work on special front tramway at T9.6.66., N.2 & 2.5 and Nos. 6.3.6 to take up tracks will be spelunker for projectors & been attacked. Work of Hill 65 continuing also supply LA PERONNE switch Tank on spoil tramways continued despite counter.	
	15		96th Coy. relieved 83rd Coy. on main lateral but 83rd Coy. remains work on tramways	
	18		84th Coy. employed in supply new switch for tracks joining BLUE & RED line on left of divisional front. Track maintenance, work of outpost line, making	
	19		small (3 men) shelters in front line. Work continues on artillery tracks. Enemy NISSEN hut at present dugouts?	
	21		Minor raid resumes.	
	23		Gas been attack from tracks on special tramway. 75 tracks on each of 3 trains. Each truck will 20 cylinders. These were discharged electrically between 2 and 3 A.M. Heavy kept in site by 83rd Coy. during the operation. All tracks were pushed back right 35' which was when tramway.	
	25		Daylight starts at ANDRES by 83rd Coy. Also tracks for munitions for at CHERISY	

A7050. Wt. W22859/M1293. 750,000. 1/7. D. D. & L., Ltd. Forms/C2118/14.

SECRET.

Army Form C. 2118.

WAR DIARY
of
INTELLIGENCE SUMMARY.
(Erase heading not required.)

H.Q. 20TH DIVISIONAL ENGINEERS

Instructions regarding War Diaries and Intelligence Summaries are contained in F. S. Regs., Part II. and the Staff Manual respectively. Title pages will be prepared in manuscript.

Place	Date	Hour	Summary of Events and Information	Remarks and references to Appendices
CHATEAU-DE-LA-HAYE	MAY 1918 28		83rd Cy relieved 96th Cy in front line. Batts. at CADENCY dugouts and MOISLEN huts taken over. Cadency are recruits at 83.170.	Sheet 44B EST. NAZMAZE RIVER
	29		Took of main kinds principal, infantry and signalling carried out at the burial RE. Dr. LENS JUNCTION. X.2.c	

Hostiler C.P.R.E. for C.R.E. 20 Divis.

SECRET　　　　　　　　　　　　　　　　　　Army Form C. 2118.

WAR DIARY
or
INTELLIGENCE SUMMARY.
(Erase heading not required)

Instructions regarding War Diaries and Intelligence Summaries are contained in F. S. Regs., Part II. and the Staff Manual respectively. Title pages will be prepared in manuscript.

H.Q. 20th Divisional Engineers

Vol 36

Place	Date	Hour	Summary of Events and Information	Remarks and references to Appendices
CHATEAU DE-LA-HAIE	JUNE 1918			
	1		83rd Field Coy. in line with Right Bde., 84th with Left 96th F. Coy. in reserve.	See 74 B & ST NAZAIRE RIVER
	2		ABLAIN-ST-NAZAIRE. Work in line on small shelter proofs for trench garrison — hby. support mining with bratton in forgery.	
	3		83rd Coy. kept lines heavy shelled bivvies temporary.	
	4		96th F. Coy. S/S at own camp, XAC, ABLAIN-ST-NAZAIRE (1 platoon area from SOUCHEZ).	
	5		"Just man" battle stations manned 3.15 P.M. and sets on Templeux and near outskirts of Companies inspected by Divisional Commander.	
	6		96th F.Coy. took over work in left Bde sector from 2nd F. Coy. Work principal on dug dugouts, hby. support shelters, communication alley O.P.'s look on RIDMONT dugouts and HILL 65	
	7		83rd Coy. started work on installation of gate cell at divisional H.Q. centre. CARENCY.	
	8		84th Coy. erected kitchen camp, &c.	
	9		83rd Coy. working on minor dugouts in LORETTE area.	
	11		Work continued on Right Bde. front on steel shelters and dugouts.	
	12			

SECRET

Army Form C. 2118.

WAR DIARY
or
INTELLIGENCE SUMMARY.
(Erase heading not required.)

H.Q. 203 Divisional Engineers

Instructions regarding War Diaries and Intelligence Summaries are contained in F.S. Regs., Part II. and the Staff Manual respectively. Title pages will be prepared in manuscript.

Place	Date	Hour	Summary of Events and Information	Remarks and references to Appendices
JUNE 1918				
CHATEAU DE LA HAIE	13		832 Cy. started work on new Rifle Range and R.A. H.Q. S.18.F.1.1.	Ship 44 B & ST NAZAIRE RIVER
	14		832 Cy. took over work in camp at X + C from 84th Cy. 612th R.E.	
			84th Cy. was to finish and 2 messing huts.	
	15		84th Cy. relieved 96th Cy. in Left Bank sector	
	16		96th Cy. relieved 832 Cy. in Rifle Range Sector. C.R.E. went on leave	
			Major LW. MASSIE, M.C. R.E. 832 Pwd Cy R.E. acting in his place	
	17		On duty 832 Cy. constrl. of pre fabs at X6c and R3+d	
	18		Fr. 6. working on Aircrk. O.P.s, shelter, M.G.S.P.	
	19		832 Cy. states in rest delivery apparat. ("ORRS DISINFECTOR")	
			at the Divisional Baths, CARENCY	
	20		Camp at X + C completed	
	21		96th Cy. runny and reclaiming old trenches. to serve to our defenses	
	23		6 OR of 96th Cy. that fired in army with 2 Lustral Rifles and delayed	
			stemmer to 6 days. 84th Cy. moved their forward field L.STORES	
			HOUSE. M.37.c.15.20	

SECRET. Army Form C. 2118.

WAR DIARY
or
INTELLIGENCE SUMMARY.

HQ. 20th Divisional Engineers

(Erase heading not required.)

Instructions regarding War Diaries and Intelligence Summaries are contained in F.S. Regs., Part II. and the Staff Manual respectively. Title pages will be prepared in manuscript.

Place	Date	Hour	Summary of Events and Information	Remarks and references to Appendices
CHATEAU DE LA HAIE	JUNE 1918 24		Major P.G. MACRAE, M.C. R.E. proceeded on leave to U.K. Capt. V.G. HALSTEAD, M.C. R.E. acting O.C. 84 F.C. 2nd Cpl R.E. 832 Cy. states many coleman Group from SOUCHEZ to ABLAIN-ST-NAZAIRE, X.3.d.	New 448 St Nazaire River
	25		83rd Cy. took over work on Ryr R.R. extn. from 96th Cy. took on communication SIDNEY - BADDECK - BLUENOSE area.	
	26		96th Cy. took over work in camp X.3.d. 19 mm. & 9 ft × 5 ft huts	
	27		wk with P.U.O. 30 to hospital	
	30		83rd Cy. continuing work in group etc.	
			Work normal	

N. Bate
Capt. R.E.
for C.R.E. 20th Division

SECRET

Army Form C. 2118.

WAR DIARY
or
INTELLIGENCE SUMMARY.
(Erase heading not required.)

H.Q. 20TH DIVISIONAL ENGINEERS

Instructions regarding War Diaries and Intelligence Summaries are contained in F. S. Regs., Part II. and the Staff Manual respectively. Title pages will be prepared in manuscript.

Place	Date	Hour	Summary of Events and Information	Remarks and references to Appendices
CHATEAU DE LA HAIE	JULY 1918			Sheet 44B LD ST. NAZAIRE RIVER
	1		83rd Fld Cy. working in Right Bde area on deep dugouts, potato shelters etc, with a platoon in reserve working on BETHUNE and GREEN line from pailes in wire entgs. 84 F. Cy. (3 sections) at M.T.A. Dump working on erecting O.P. cover, from pack matls. shells (mostly 4.5" wk B.L.P. pack) and machine gun emplacements. Relief of 83 Cy. heavy B.P. shelves being built. Wire dumps around Cavalier. 96th Cy. – were having.
	2		96th Cy. from 3.F. work allotted to Ref. Fld. Store
	3		work as above
	4		96 F. Cy. took over work in Left Bde. area from 84 Cy.
	5		96th Cy. working on concrete pill box posts, O.P.s, M.G. emplacements and portable small fright shelters, for occupation.
	6		
	7		84 F. Cy. employed dismantling COLUMBIA camp and many huts and weekly at M.26.d.3.d. (MERICOURT–ST–NAZAIRE) Refuges & MARQUEFFLE'S Rifle Range
	8		work as above
	9		
	10		
	14		84 F. Cy. commenced work on reserve H.Q. for Left Brigade at M.26.d.7.3. New system of affoibement of work to Fld Companies announced. (see...

SECRET Army Form C. 2118.

WAR DIARY
INTELLIGENCE SUMMARY.
(Erase heading not required.)

HQ. 10th DIVISIONAL ENGINEERS

Place	Date	Hour	Summary of Events and Information	Remarks and references to Appendices
CHATEAU DE LA-HAIE WNC	July 1918 14.		Company taking charge of a hutts and armmaft its own water supplies of Brigadier. 83rd Coy information to the Right half of Southern Burned Boundary; the found report line the boundary in the southern extending from the Brown Line of the direction East the main extending from the Brown line of the Flowed area to the 6:00 at about 15:30, there the bottom edge of the Flowed area to the found line of Bowneta to the wilt and the Brown line in the bottom 96 Co. infamation the Authoritin; the wire binded by the southern untouched and further edge of flowed area to the North the flood water there of Bowneta on the East; the Lens-Lievin road (exclusive) in the butt and the Brown line in the butt; Lens-Lievin road (southern) in the butt, 84 Co. information for Right half; Lens-Lievin road (southern) in the butt, found water line of Bowneta in the East, Northern boundary of the butt and Brown line in the butt.	Sketch B and ST. NAZAIRE WOOD
	15 16		253 Co. making a recover for pit in half acres, found rock in yards water built to pump water-Nearpipe through shelter & connect Extn. mouth to half- nouth.	

SECRET.

Army Form C. 2118.

WAR DIARY
or
INTELLIGENCE SUMMARY.
(Erase heading not required.)

HQ 20th DIVISIONAL ENGINEERS

Instructions regarding War Diaries and Intelligence Summaries are contained in F. S. Regs., Part II. and the Staff Manual respectively. Title pages will be prepared in manuscript.

Place	Date	Hour	Summary of Events and Information	Remarks and references to Appendices
	JULY 1918			Book 448 to ST NAZAIRE RIVER
CHATEAU-DE LA-HAIE	17		Work on enemy O.P.s and front entails of of a material nature were done.	
	18		Work normal	
	19			
	20			
	21			
	22		No Germans took part in parties with our German Comdr. of RE.	
	23		2 O.R. wounded (cavalry)	
	24		Work normal	
	25			
	26		9 C of E ates into line between mist ad MBEC; reporting back Camp? by trucks tonight to HINGES Cant.	
	27		Work normal. Cannot read my diary.	
	28			
	29			
	30			
	31			

W.T.C.L
Lt. Col. RE
for CRE 20th Divn.

SECRET

WAR DIARY
INTELLIGENCE SUMMARY
(Erase heading not required.)

Army Form C. 2118.

H.Q. 20TH DIVISIONAL ENGINEERS

Vol 36

Instructions regarding War Diaries and Intelligence Summaries are contained in F.S. Regs., Part II. and the Staff Manual respectively. Title pages will be prepared in manuscript.

Place	Date	Hour	Summary of Events and Information	Remarks and references to Appendices
CHATEAU-DE-LA-HAIE	AUGUST 1918			
	1		83rd Fd Coy, 2 sections working in 60th Bde. area (AVION sector), mainly deep dugout protection, field shelters and drainage. 2 sections on reserve gun pits and camp work. 84th Fd Coy working on left subsector (LENS sector), 2 shelters, improving 2 tunnels OP's for RFA. Creating trench gun pits and overhead cover, new shelter, making a HENICOURT dump. 96th Fd Coy working on certain subsectors (LENS sector), shelter, firing nodding in concrete platform pits, new bivi for crazy pave shelter, and concrete OP. 96th Fd Coy found blocks road to ANGRES M33 d 1.7	Sheet 44B 44A 51C 51B
	2		"Zulu" man battle station carried out 10 p.m.	
	4		Visit of H.M. the King to Chateau de la Haie. Reported 10am first line. H.Q. personnel lined the road.	
	8			
	10		Look normal.	
	12		Strenuous patterns being prepared for all tunnel areas.	
	14/15		Division took over MERICOURT sector from 8th Division. 83rd Fd Coy relieved by	
			11th Field Coy R.E. Division entering a 3-brigade front.	
	16		Look normal. Climatic character of new work. Good clear trench system in good order.	
	17		2nd Fd Coy rested in time of 1 officer 1 NCO 5 OR labour at Right Group RFA artillery 83rd Coy 1 feet bridge 96th 1 third.	
	20		96th Fd Coy took over work from 83rd Fd Coy in certain sectors, including HIRONDELLE depot.	

SECRET.

WAR DIARY
or
INTELLIGENCE SUMMARY.
(Erase heading not required.)

HQ. 20TH DIVISIONAL ENGINEERS

Army Form C. 2118.

Instructions regarding War Diaries and Intelligence Summaries are contained in F. S. Regs., Part II. and the Staff Manual respectively. Title pages will be prepared in manuscript.

Place	Date	Hour	Summary of Events and Information	Remarks and references to Appendices
CHATEAU-DE-LA-HAIE	AUGUST 1918			
	21		96th Coy 2 sections working on pillboxes, artillery OP, shelter, RAP and ADS	Skeff 44.B 44.A 51.C 51.B
	22		84th Coy supplied 3 sappers for road works, charges successfully fired. Aeroplane service proposed	
	23		6th Borders front, LENS Rd., handed over to 24th Divn. 84th Coy handed over work in this area, except OP in ST. PIERRE, to 103rd Field Coy RE	
	27		Divn. HQ and ACHEVILLE sector from 5th Divn. and killed on LENS front taken over	
			84th Coy. 96th Coy supplied 5 sappers for road 10 O.R. wounded	
	28		84th Coy relieved 223rd Coy in ACHEVILLE Sector. HQ at La TARGETTE. Front wire the front. LC 530.c.5.55. Reversed a parapet trench & RE plant, making shelters and	
	31		not moved.	

W. Cole
Capt. RE
[signature] 20th Divn.

WAR DIARY

SECRET

INTELLIGENCE SUMMARY
(Erase heading not required)

H.Q. 20TH DIVISIONAL ENGINEERS

Army Form C. 2118.

Stamp: COMMANDING ROYAL ENGINEER 30 SEP 1918 20TH DIVISIONAL ENGINEERS

Vol 39

Place	Date	Hour	Summary of Events and Information	Remarks and references to Appendices
Château de la Haie	September 1918			Sheets 44A, 44B, 51B, 51C
	1		Expects German retirement on divisional front. 1st & 2nd Tunnelling Cos. about to be taken in reserve to be freed with extra and kept ready to lead to mines and booby traps.	
	2		83rd Coy. working in MERICOURT Sector. 1st & 2nd ACHEVILLE Sector. 96th Coy. AVION Sector. Each with 2 Sections forward and 2 in reserve working camps etc. Principal work is line dugouts, elementary chambers, battle maintenance and demolitions.	
	3		83rd Coy. working on new trainage arrangements at divisional Baths CHERISY	
	4,5		83rd Coy. working on recovery of LENS-ARRAS road. 83rd Coy. Batt'n mess hut (2 missions) at ALBERTA Camp. 96th Coy. erected camouflage AVIGNY-GIVENCHY rd S4c & S11c	
	7		84th Coy. repairing NEW BRUNSWICK ROAD. 96th Coy. Lyric pillbox for MOIR pillbox M30c9.1. Trainage of camp progressing 96th Coy. receiving stores near La COROTTE for found roads driven from S4c & S11c, adapted as from OPEN CT.	
	8			
	11			

SECRET Army Form C. 2118.

WAR DIARY
INTELLIGENCE SUMMARY.
(Erase heading not required.)

H.Q. 26TH DIVISIONAL ENGINEERS

Instructions regarding War Diaries and Intelligence Summaries are contained in F. S. Regs., Part II. and the Staff Manual respectively. Title pages will be prepared in manuscript.

Place	Date	Hour	Summary of Events and Information	Remarks and references to Appendices
	September 1917			sheet ff
Château de la Haie	11		Camouflage LENS-ARRAS Road completed from S.12.d.6.8. to S.24.c.6.8. By 83rd Coy.	44 A
	12		83rd Coy. completed Boyeffles Visual Station.	44 B
	13		Hot normal. Much damage, dugouts and shelters in the line. Each Coy. with one Section employing its men training for a week in trench drill.	57 B
	14		Fo.E.G. completed R.D.S. at B.2.a.9.5. Road at NEW COLUMBIA Camp being made up.	57 C
	16		96th Coy. with 1 Section wired in training area at MAROEUFFLES	
	18		Change being witnessed from old mines and returned to training. R.E. Park, LENS JUNCTION	
	20		83rd Coy. camped out upstream of YMCA hut CARENCY, due to shell fire. Pioneers working on KINGSTON ROAD with material from PARIS 3	
	22		Work normal. 96th Coy. constructed chlorinating chamber near PARIS 6	

SECRET

Army Form C. 2118.

WAR DIARY
&
INTELLIGENCE SUMMARY.

H.Q. 20th DIVISIONAL ENGINEERS

(Erase heading not required.)

Instructions regarding War Diaries and Intelligence Summaries are contained in F.S. Regs., Part II. and the Staff Manual respectively. Title pages will be prepared in manuscript.

Place	Date	Hour	Summary of Events and Information	Remarks and references to Appendices
	September 1918.			
Chateau de la Haie	24		Batt. HQ dugout at T.13 a.1.7 complete and having internal fittings put in & finishing etc.	See a 77A 77B 57B 57C
	25		All Companies making complete tunnel and dugout anchors for accommodation.	
	26		Road work & tunneling continued.	
			11 Lt A. GORDON, 6th K.R.R. attached during month to Coy. for Intermediate Mining	

Walsh
Capt. R.E.
for C.R.E. 20th Divn

SECRET

Army Form C. 2118.

Instructions regarding War Diaries and Intelligence Summaries are contained in F. S. Regs., Part II. and the Staff Manual respectively. Title pages will be prepared in manuscript.

WAR DIARY
or
INTELLIGENCE SUMMARY.
(Erase heading not required.)

HQ 20th Divisional Engineers

Place	Date	Hour	Summary of Events and Information	Remarks and references to Appendices
CHATEAU-DE-LA-HAIE	October 1918			Dec/s
	1		Airfields practised on 14 days bombing + CRE (i) M.A. Gordon, 6th X.S.I. batty	LDn 2/LB, 7th B, 12th B, 51st B, 51st C
	2		Field companies and mounted	
	3		Enemy withdraws again on divisional front. Field companies all working	
	4		on repairs of forward roads.	
	5		Relieved by RE Brown.	
VILLERS CAUCHEL	6		HQ and 83rd, 84th Fld Coys CHATEL (manuscript), 83rd Fd Coy at ESTREES CAUCHIE, 84th and 96th Fd Coys at BETHENCOURT	
	7-29		Divisional Pontoon details and trestle trucks now being on Fd companies	
	16		kept loaned from RE UK.	
	30		83rd Fd Coy entrained for CAMBRAI.	
CAMBRAI	31		84th HQ moved by road and joined 1st CAMBRAI (VIII Corps 3rd Army)	not VIII Corps 71
			84th and 96th Fd Coys entrained for CAMBRAI	
			Major J.N. MADDEN MC RE left to R.E.R.G.H.Q. RE to take over as 2nd in com	
			Captain M.C.I.R.E.	
			The Indicate joined HQ HLG Fm 83rd = 3rd Cyclo	

/signature/

SECRET.

Army Form C. 2118.

WAR DIARY
or
INTELLIGENCE SUMMARY.
(Erase heading not required.)

H.Q. 20TH DIVISIONAL ENGINEERS

Place	Date	Hour	Summary of Events and Information	Remarks and references to Appendices
	NOVEMBER 1918			See WAR-DIARIES
CAMBRAI	1		Div HQ and all Fd. Coy. HQs in CAMBRAI	
NESCHES-LEZ-AUBERT	3		Divn. moved to NESCHES-LEZ-AUBERT. 11th Coy to "Pont" forts — 83rd Coy to VERDIGIES. 84. & 229. Coy to ST AUBERT	
VERDIGIES	6		Divn moved to VERDIGIES. 83. Coy to SEPMERIES. 84. & 229. Coy to VERDIGIES	
	7		C.R.E. WAR. BOURNE reports for duty. 11. 84. & 229. Bldg. R.E. 83rd Coy moved to JENLAIN. Ph E. SEPMERIES. 96th & VERDIGIES	
MARGNIES-LE-GRAND	8		Divn HQ moved to MARGNIES-LE-GRAND. 83rd Coy to ST MART at VILLERS EN E. Coy to MARGNIES LE PETIT. 11 E. Coy to JENLAIN.	
BAVAI	9		Divn. HQ moved to BAVAI. 83rd Coy moved to FEIGNIES	
	10		84th Coy moved to FEIGNIES. 96th Coy moved to ST MART LA MALLE	
HIGNIES	11		Armistice concluded with Germans to take effect from 11.0, 11th November 83rd Coy moved to GOEGNIES-CHAUSSÉE. 84. E. Coy & R.27 G.G.G (N.R. Send SM MAUBERGE). 96 E. Coy K. GOEGNIES-CHAUSSÉE.	
	12		Work in hand — filling in bridge craters etc. to enable trunk army to advance into Germany.	
	-19		were found in 17.	

SECRET

Army Form C. 2118.

WAR DIARY
or
INTELLIGENCE SUMMARY.
(Erase heading not required.)

H.Q. 20TH DIVISIONAL ENGINEERS

Instructions regarding War Diaries and Intelligence Summaries are contained in F. S. Regs., Part II and the Staff Manual respectively. Title pages will be prepared in manuscript.

Place	Date	Hour	Summary of Events and Information	Remarks and references to Appendices
	NOVEMBER 1918			
PEIGNIES	22nd		Field Companies and Their Bivouac Coys as follows: 83rd F. Coy. at BELLIGNIES/VILLERCIES	Shot 12
			84th F. Coy. at PEIGNIES, 96th F. Coy. at TAISNIERES	
MARGNIES LE GRAND	23rd		Divn. HQ. and 84th F. Coy. to MARGNIES-LE-GRAND. 83rd F. Coy. to BRY.	
			84th F. Coy. to ST. WAAST-LA-VALLÉE. 96th F. Coy. to MARGNIES-LE-PETIT.	
	24th		83rd F. Coy. moved to SOMMAING. 84th F. Coy. to MARGNIES-LE-PETIT, 96th F. to	
			F. Coy. to ST. MARTIN	
	25th		83rd F. Coy. moved to MATHIES-LEZ-ABBOTT, 84th F. to VENDEGIES, 96th to ST. VAAST	
RIEUX	26th		Divn HQ. moved to RIEUX.	
	27th		HQ. R.E. and 2 Section 83rd Field Coy. R.E. moved to to PAS-EN-ARTOIS.	Shot LEWIS 11
			Remainder 83rd F. Coy. moved to and 83rd F. HQ. at PANCHEMONT, 84th F. Coy. moved to	
			CACHENELES, 96th F. Coy. to COURSET	
	28th		Advance reconnaissance of PAS area for accommodation for Division on route	
			to Germany.	
	30th		96th Field Coy. arrived at PANCHEMONT & Coy.	

W.R.E.
C.R.R.E.
for C.R.E. 20th Division

SECRET

Army Form C. 2118.

WAR DIARY
or
INTELLIGENCE SUMMARY.
(Erase heading not required)

83rd Field Co. RE

VALENCIENNES Hiscock Sheet 12

Place	Date	Hour	Summary of Events and Information	Remarks and references to Appendices
CAMBRAI	1st		Sector training all day. O.C. & 2ID I/C getting pontooning reconnoitre bridging Ply at PROVILLE 58.59.	
	2nd		No 2 Sec. + 1/2 of No 1 { at PROVILLE. V2 O.C. visits C.R.E. Received orders midnight for move next day	
			No 3 " do reconning bridge at will	
			No 4 sect.	
	3rd		Co. reported with 60th Bde. Group to RIEUX 45.84. O.C. to IWUY 4D.9.8. to reconnoitre bridging P.T.I.	
	4th		Co. moved to VENDEGIES - weather bad - billets bad. Lieut HUNT rejoined from leave 39.1.2.	
	5th		Remained at VENDEGIES. C.R.E. called.	
	6th		Co. marched to SEPMERIES 39.8.4.	
	7th		Co. reconnoitring to JENLAIN 3.H.6.8. No billets. 81st 46.Co. closed up 4 walls down.	
			"Lieut. Twitchett returned from hospital." to Lt. WAET 3J.0.7. Very bad road abroad blocked with traffic.	
	8th		Co. marched 24th Div. tree of half required to complete elevation at 3J.10.64.	
			O.C. visited C.R.E. No half required.	
			O.C. to 60th + 72nd Bdes + 129 4D.Co. at 32.6.5.	
	9th		Co. moved to TEIGNIES 3L.0.6. Nos 1 & 3 Secs superseding 2 craters on	
	10th		2 officers out all day reconnoitring roads. No 2 Sec. MAUBEUGE - MONS road. No 1 Sec. Marked 2 craters at 21.2.0. Civilians employed on all craters. O.C. to conference with C.R.E. at FEIGNIES at 10.00. No 3 Sec. worked in relief all night.	
	11th		No 1 Sec. finished work. No 3 Sec. continued work. No 4 Sec. to No 2 new craters at GOEGNIES CHAUSSÉE 2L.50.15. Co. moved to Chau. de ROGERIE 2L.18.63.	

Sheet 2

Army Form C. 2118.

WAR DIARY
or
INTELLIGENCE SUMMARY.
(Erase heading not required.)

Instructions regarding War Diaries and Intelligence Summaries are contained in F.S. Regs., Part II. and the Staff Manual respectively. Title pages will be prepared in manuscript.

Place	Date	Hour	Summary of Events and Information	Remarks and references to Appendices
	12th		Materials obtained for building 20 metres at GOEGNIES CHAUSSÉE – Orders received to fill in craters. Began fill 1100.	
	13th		Work continued	
	14th		Both craters at GOEGNIES CHAUSSÉE taken over by 177 Tny Co. R.E., existing work pulled down & re-erected.	
	15th		Work continued on two craters at 2L.2.D. Remainder of Co. went to	
	16th		Orders received for repair of culvert at FEIGNIES. Dugouts pits.	
	17th		No 4 Sec commenced work on culvert at FEIGNIES	
	18th		IVth Army commenced forward march.	
	22nd		Co. march to BELLIGNIES 3J.3.9. & joined 60th Bde. Group.	
			No 4 Sec. remained at FEIGNIES to complete culvert.	
	23rd		Co. march with 60th Bde. to BRY 3I.1.8.	
	24th		Co. march to SOMMAINS 39.0.2. No 4 Sec rejoined from BELLIGNIES leaving marching stage from FEIGNIES on the 23rd.	
	25th		Co. march to AVESNE LEZ AUBERT 46.6.4.	
	26th		Did not move. G.O.C. 60th Bde visited Co. in morning. O.C. 2½ to E.P.E.	

Sheet 3

WAR DIARY
or
INTELLIGENCE SUMMARY.
(Erase heading not required.)

Army Form C. 2118.

Place	Date	Hour	Summary of Events and Information	Remarks and references to Appendices
	27th		Transport + 2 sections marched to BOURFIES arriving 1900 - into billets 55.A.4.7. Hq. + 2 sections by bus to FAMECHON (LENS Sheet 11, 5F.65.72.)	
	28th		Transport + 2 sections marched to BIENVILLERS + found 20th D.G.	
	29th		Transport + 2 sections arrived at FAMECHON. Orders recd. to detail one section for work at VAUCHELLE CAMP 5F.7.1.	
	30th		O.C. reconnoitred work at VAUCHELLE and HENU water point.	
			Officers O.Rs	
			Reinforcements during month Nil 9	
			Casualties Nil Nil	
			Co. strength beginning of month 7 201	
			Co. strength end of month 7 208	

H.O.P. Heazewoff/Maj/R.E.
O/c yield 10 P.R.
O.E. 83

Army Form C. 2118.

WAR DIARY
INTELLIGENCE SUMMARY.
(Erase heading not required).

HQ. 20TH DIVISIONAL ENGINEERS

Sheet LENS 11

Place	Date	Hour	Summary of Events and Information	Remarks and references to Appendices
PAS	December 1916 1		HQ. at PAS. HQ. & Field Companies at FAMECHON. Work on Camp and Huts in Divisional area by Working parties. Field Engs. continued work on details at HQ., principally water, baths and floors. R.CM. HORSE, A&E. RE. proceeded on leave to UK 23/4/16. Christmas holidays.	
	25 -27			
	28 -31		Work continued as above.	

Vaile
Capt RE
for CRE. 20 Division

Hd qr 2nd Australian Divisional R.E. SHEET 1

Army Form C. 2118.

WAR DIARY
or
INTELLIGENCE SUMMARY.
(Erase heading not required.)

Place	Date	Hour	Summary of Events and Information	Remarks and references to Appendices
P.A.S.	January 1919			
	1st		Field Companies employed improving accommodation for all ranks in the Divisional Area.	
			Signal Company improving their own accommodation.	
	2nd		Lieut H DONALDSON posted from 30th Divisional Signal Co R.E. to 63rd R.G.A Signal Subsection.	E.M.N
	3rd		Companies employed as above, in addition 30th Divisional Signal Co R.E.	
	4th		Laying Cable	E.M.N
	5th		As above. Captain H.E.L. PORTER MC 30th Divisional Signal Co R.E. for Demobilization	E.M.N
			12 O.R's from Field Co. H.O.R's from Signal Co. left to be demobilized.	E.M.N
	6th		Companies employed as above. C.R.E. (Lieut. Col. E.M. NEWELL) returned from leave in U.K.	E.M.N
	7th		Companies employed as above.	
	13th		Lieut G.S. BRIDGMAN left 7th Field Co to be demobilized. 23 O.R's from Field Co.	E.M.N
	14th		Companies employed as above 13 O.R's from Field Co left for demobilization. 8 O.R's from Signal left for demobilization	E.M.N
	15th		do 18 O.R's from Field Co & O.R's from Signal left for demobilization.	E.M.N

WAR DIARY
INTELLIGENCE SUMMARY
(Erase heading not required.)

Army Form C. 2118.

SHEET 2.

C.R.E.

Place	Date	Hour	Summary of Events and Information	Remarks and references to Appendices
PAS-	January 1919			
	16th to 18th		Companies employed as above.	
			Requisitioned Lieut Major S. GREEN left Head Quarters to be demobilised.	
			1st O.R. from Field Coy. 7. O.R. from Signal Coy left to be demobilised.	
	19th		Lieutenant F.H. POOLE M.C. left 93rd Field Coy R.E. To be demobilised.	EMW
	20th to 22nd		Companies employed as above. 1 O.R. left 93rd Field Coy R.E to be demobilised	EMW
			do —	
			2.O.R's left Signal Coy to be demobilised. Lieutenant R.S. CORK left 96th Field	
	23rd to 25th		Coy to be demobilised. C.R.E attended conference at C.E. XVII Corps Offices RE Demualisation Personnel in RE.	EMW
			Companies employed as above.	
			Captain H.W. COALES. Adjutant Commenced R.E. left Head Quarters to be demobilised	EMW
	26th		1 O.R. from Head Quarters 2 O.R's from Field Coy, 1 O.R from Signal Coy left to be demobilised	EMW
	27th		Companies employed as above. 2 1. O.R from Field Coy. left to be demobilised.	EMW
	28th		do —	
	29th		2nd Lieut G. BROWN left 97th Field Coy and 7 O.R from Field Coys left to be demobilised.	EMW
	30th 31st		Companies employed as above.	EMW
			do —	

C.W. Newell Lieut & C.R.E.
C.R.E. 20th Division

Head Quarters 80th Divisional R.E.

Army Form C. 2118.

WAR DIARY
INTELLIGENCE SUMMARY.
(Erase heading not required.)

Place	Date	Hour	Summary of Events and Information	Remarks and references to Appendices
PAS	February 1919			
	1st		Field Companies employed improving accommodation for all units in the Divisional Area. 96th Field Co. R.E. laid out and erected Nissen huts to accommodate R.A.S.C. and guards for wagons and guns to be placed near MONDICOURT Railway Station.	E.M.S.
	3rd		Signal Coy. laying cable in the Divisional area. Men proceeded to Concentration Camp for demobilization. 93rd Field Co. R.E. 8, 84th Field Co. R.E. 5, 96th Field Co. R.E. 10.	E.M.S.
	11th		93rd Field Co. R.E. commenced work at BUS-LES-ARTOIS repairing the MAIRIE, repairing wells and erecting a cattle shelter, to cancel claims made for damage. 96th Field Co. R.E. instructed to supervise loading and horse standings near MONDICOURT Railway Station for the use of 60 1/8 Field Ambulance.	E.M.S.
	12th		84th Field Co. R.E. instructed to build stablings for 100 horses of the R.A.S.C. Divisional Train at AUTHIEULE. C.R.E. visited the site with 2nd Lieut. D. CAMPION 84th Field Co. R.E. and permitted work to be done.	E.M.S.
	14th		Men proceeded to Concentration Camp for demobilization. H.Qrs. 5th Lieut A. GORDON attached from 6th K.S.L.I. 93rd Field Co. R.E. 4, 84th Field Co. R.E. 6, 96th Field Co. R.E. 12.	E.M.S.

Map. Sht LENS 11
1/100,000

HEAD QUARTERS 20TH Divisional R.E.

WAR DIARY
or
INTELLIGENCE SUMMARY.
(Erase heading not required.)

Army Form C. 2118.

SHEET 2

Instructions regarding War Diaries and Intelligence
Summaries are contained in F. S. Regs., Part II.
and the Staff Manual respectively. Title pages
will be prepared in manuscript.

Place	Date	Hour	Summary of Events and Information	Remarks and references to Appendices
PAS	February 1919			
	15TH		96TH Field Company instructed to repair loading platforms and approaches at MONDICOURT Railway Station	GW
	16TH		Men proceeded to Concentration Camps for demobilisation, Head Quarters & 96TH Field Co. R.E. #	GW
	21st		83rd Field Co. R.E. 3 84TH Field Co. R.E. # 96TH Field Co. R.E. #	GW
			Men proceeded to Concentration Camp for demobilisation. 83rd Field Co. R.E. #	GW
			84TH Field Co. R.E. 11 96TH Field Co. R.E. 2	GW
	22nd		84TH Field Co. R.E. instructed to erect an additional Nissen hut for the Machine Gun Batalion at MARIEUX.	GW
	24TH		84TH Field Co. R.E. completed work erecting & stabling at AUTHIEULE for R.A.S.C.	GW
			84TH Field Co. R.E. commenced to re-erect fencing in land belonging to the Château at ACHEUX, in settlement of a claim.	GW
	27TH		Draft of 10 NCOs proceeded to Field Companies of the 41st Division from 83rd Field Co. R.E. 3	GW
			84TH Field Co. R.E. 2 96TH Field Co. R.E. 5	GW
			Men proceeded to Concentration Camps for demobilisation 83rd Field Co. R.E. 6 84TH Field Co. R.E. 14	GW
	28TH		83rd Field Co. R.E. employed on repair work at BUS, and COIN 84TH Field Co. R.E. employed	GW
			repairing WARLINCOURT road installation, erecting TANGY'S oil engine at P.A.S. of 96TH Field Co. R.E. employed repairing sheds at railway sidings and approaches at MONDICOURT.	GW

E.K. Newall Lieut. Co. R.E.
C.R.E. 20TH Division

War Sheet LENS, 11
1/100,000

HEAD QUARTERS 20TH (S) DIVISIONAL R.E.
WAR DIARY
SHEET 1.

Army Form C. 2118.

INTELLIGENCE SUMMARY
(Erase heading not required.)

Place	Date	Hour	Summary of Events and Information	Remarks and references to Appendices
PAS	MARCH 1919			
	1st		Field Companies employed carrying out minor repairs to buildings and generally in the Divisional area to make good damage and loss numerous claims submitted by civilians withdrawn	
	2nd		2nd Lieutenant G.E.A. GREENSILL left the 84th Field Company R.E. to report to C.R.E. CALAIS for duty under Director of Works	
	4th		2nd Lieutenant E.J. HOAR left the 84th Field Company R.E. to report to C.R.E. BOULOGNE for duty under Director of Works	
	7th		Captain R.H. HODGSON joined from the 50th (S) Divisional R.E. and took over command of the 83rd Field Co R.E. vice Major T.W. HAYCRAFT who left the Company last December & proceeded to Chatham on a course of Instruction	
			Draft of 33 men from Field Companies left to join the 30th Divisional R.E. in the Army of Occupation. 2nd Lieut W.N. COOK of 96th Field Co. went as conducting officer	
	10th		2 men from 84th Field Co. R.E. proceeded to the Corps Concentration Camp for demobilization. Men proceeded to Concentration Camp for demobilization H. Qrs. 1, 83rd Field Co. R.E. 4, 84th Field Co. R.E. 10, 96th Field Co R.E. 3	
			No. 48534 Sapper R. WINSTANLEY 96th Field Co. R.E. attached to H.Qrs. re-enlisted for 3 years	
	15th		Commenced Great RETIREMENT at MONDICOURT	

Map: LENS 11
1/100,000

HEAD QUARTERS 30th Divisional R.E.
WAR DIARY
INTELLIGENCE SUMMARY
(Erase heading not required.)

Army Form C. 2118.
SHEET 2

Instructions regarding War Diaries and Intelligence Summaries are contained in F. S. Regs., Part II. and the Staff Manual respectively. Title pages will be prepared in manuscript.

Place	Date	Hour	Summary of Events and Information	Remarks and references to Appendices
	MARCH 1919			
PAS.	17th		Sold 3 huts at TOUTENCOURT for 1600 Francs, 1800 Francs and one corrugated iron shelter at BERTRANCOURT for 70 Francs. E.W.N.	
	18th		Ordered 83rd Field Co. R.E. to make all preparations and close down the pumping station at ACHEUX, and be relieved by this Division. E.W.N.	
	21st		Major E.B. HUGH-JONES, M.C. and Lieutenant W.N. COOK of the 96th Field Co. R.E. and 1 man from H.Qrs. leave from 83rd Field Co. R.E., 12 men from 84th Field Co. R.E. and 11 men from 96th Field Co. R.E. proceeded to Corps Concentration Camp for demobilization. E.W.N.	
	22nd 23rd		Sold 4 huts at TOUTENCOURT for 650 Francs, 500 Francs, 1400 Francs and 850 Francs. E.W.N.	
			96th Field Co. R.E. took in hand repairs to wells in GRENAS and POMMERA. E.W.N.	
	25th		2nd Lieutenant P. TRIPLETE left the 84th Field Co. R.E. to report to A.D.E.S., DOULLENS on being No. 10 degrees b.d. Easton. E.W.N.	
	28th		Hqrs proceeded to Concentration Camp. 83rd Field Co. R.E. 84th Field Co. R.E. 96th Field Co. R.E. 2. 83rd Field Co. R.E. took in hand repairs to farm of some which had been occupied by D.A.D.O.S. at ACHEUX Chateau and stained with paraffin. E.W.N.	
	29th		83rd Field Co. R.E. instructed to repair a well at ST AMAND to cancel a claim sent in by a civilian; and to dismantle the baths at COUIN. E.W.N.	

Map Sheet. LENS 11
1/100,000.

HEAD QUARTERS 20TH Divisional R.E.
WAR DIARY
INTELLIGENCE SUMMARY

SHEET 3.

Army Form C. 2118.

Instructions regarding War Diaries and Intelligence Summaries are contained in F. S. Regs., Part II. and the Staff Manual respectively. Title pages will be prepared in manuscript.

(Erase heading not required.)

Place	Date	Hour	Summary of Events and Information	Remarks and references to Appendices
PAS	MARCH 1919			
	31st		96TH Field Co. R.E. dismantled spray bath at smithies at TOUTENCOURT and returned them to stores at R.E. Park, WARLINCOURT.	
			Sold two huts at TOUTENCOURT, 900 Francs and 400 Francs.	
			Field Companies reduced to Cadre "A" strength during the month with the exception of a first rate absent on leave and a draft of 12 men detailed to proceed to the 41ST LONDON Division to maintain — maintain —	
			Repair work to render good damage in various villages carried out during the month as far as men are available.	
			R.E. stores and materials collected and returned to R.E. Parks and Dumps.	E.N.N.
			Wagons parked at the major parks MONDICOURT.	

E. N. Newell
Lieut. Col. R.E.
C.R.E. 20TH Division.

Major Blair
× LENS. 1k 1/100,000

HEAD QUARTERS, 20TH (S)ivisional R.E.
WAR DIARY
Army Form C. 2118.
SHEET 1

INTELLIGENCE SUMMARY.
(Erase heading not required).

Instructions regarding War Diaries and Intelligence Summaries are contained in F. S. Regs., Part II. and the Staff Manual respectively. Title pages will be prepared in manuscript.

Place	Date	Hour	Summary of Events and Information	Remarks and references to Appendices
P.A.S.	APRIL 1919			91 46
	1		(1) Draft of 18 R.E. left to join the H/F LONDON (S)ivision. 8 from 83rd Field Co. R.E. 2 from 84th Field Co. R.E. and 8 from 96th Field Co. R.E.	
			A/Captain J.E. BIRD left the 84th Field Co. R.E. proceeding with 24th Base Park H. Sn. E.W.T.	
	2		Commenced moving spare stores and material from the R.E. Workshop P.A.S. to the R.E. Park WARLINCOURT.	
			Major W.A.R. BOURNE proceeded to CALAIS to come to ENGLAND on the 3rd inst. for 8 days leave. E.W.T.	
	3		84th Field Co R.E. sent in to them H.Qrs. a Telegram received from R.E. 8d. Area ordering 2nd Lieut. D. CAMPION to proceed to No 4 Workshop Company, went to C.E. 2nd A/Lt., 2nd Lieut. D. CAMPION not available being on leave of 84th Field Co. R.E.	
			Brig. Gen. DANN commanding 20th (D)ivisional Cadent inspected Transport at the wagon and gun park at MONDICOURT. E.W.T.	
	4		Men proceeded to (D)ispersal Camp for (D)emobilization from 88th Field Co. R.E. 1. 96th Field Co. R.E. 1 attached to H. Sn. from 96th Field Co. R.E. Sapper R. WINSTANLEY for 3 months re-enlistment furlough.	
			Paid 400 double gun pickets for 1400 Francs.	E.W.T.

D. D. & L., London, E.C.
(A10260) Wt W5300/P713 750,000 2/18 Sch. 52 Forms/C2118/16.

Map Sheet LENS II
1/100,000

HEAD QUARTERS 80th Division R.E.
WAR DIARY

SHEET 2.

Army Form C. 2118.

INTELLIGENCE SUMMARY.

(Erase heading not required.)

Instructions regarding War Diaries and Intelligence Summaries are contained in F.S. Regs., Part II. and the Staff Manual respectively. Title pages will be prepared in manuscript.

Place	Date	Hour	Summary of Events and Information	Remarks and references to Appendices
PAS	APRIL 1919			
	5		Clearing stores and material from R.E. Workshop PAS and sending same to No 6. R.E. Park WARLINCOURT. EWN	
	6		CRE's two chargers Class X, sent to Third Army Animal Collecting Camp at CANDAS, two new War Class "Z" horses issued in exchange. EWN	
	7		Lieutenant A. McN. HAY, of the 63rd Field Co. R.E. proceeded to 144 T.D. A T Co R.E. for duty as Adjutant R.E. a Sub. Area in the Clearing up Army. EWN	
	9th		24th Field Co. R.E. completed repairs to a farm, to cancel a claim for damage submitted by the civilian owner. EWN	
	11.		Driver BIRCHENOUGH left R.E. Head Quarters and proceeded to the Corps. Concentration Camp for demobilization. EWN	
	15.		Lieutenant H.M. GENOCHIO of the 63rd Field Co. R.E., took Temporary command of the 64th Field Co. R.E. to release 2nd Lieutenant D. CAMPION ordered to proceed to the Army of the RHINE; Major BOURNE being absent on leave. EWN. 2nd Lieutenant D. CAMPION left the 64th Field Co. R.E. and proceeded to the Army of the RHINE. EWN	
	18		1 Driver from H.Qrs. R.E.; 3 O.Rs from 63rd Field Co. R.E.; 3 O.Rs from 64th Field Co. R.E.; and 2 O.Rs from the 96th Field Co. R.E. proceeded to form the 41st LONDON Division Field Co. R.E. proceeded to the Corps 2 Q.Min from 63rd Concentration Camp for demobilization. EWN	

Map Sheet LENS 11
1/100,000

HEAD QUARTERS 20TH Divisional R.E.
WAR DIARY
or
INTELLIGENCE SUMMARY.
(Erase heading not required.)

SHEET 3.

Army Form C. 2118.

Place	Date	Hour	Summary of Events and Information	Remarks and references to Appendices
P.A.S.	25.		1 Man from the 84th Field Co. R.E. and 1 Man from the 96th Field Co. R.E. proceeded to the Corps Concentration Camp for demobilization.	
			Field Companies employed during the month clearing and repairing wells at ST AMAND, HUMBERCAMP, LACAUCHIE, GRENAS, and POMMERA.	E.M.N.

E. M. Newell
Lieut. Col. R.E.
C.R.E. 20th Division.

20th Division.
R.E.

History of R.E.

No. 3

Div. R.E.

H.Q & units.

20TH DIVISIONAL ENGINEERS.

CHANGES IN PERSONNEL.

Headquarters.

C.R.E.	From.	Date. To.	Adjutant.	From. Date. To.
Colonel. E.R. KENYON. C.B.	July. 1914.	March. 1916.	Capt. C.S. REID.	
Lt. Col. A. ROLLAND. D.S.O.	March. 1916.	June . 1917.	Capt. I.W. MASSIE. M.C.	Novr.1916. November.1916
Lt. Col. E.M. NEWELL. D.S.O.	June. 1917.		Lt. H.E. HILL. M.C.	Nov.1916. October. 1917.
			Capt. H.W. COALES.M.C.	Oct. 1917. Jan. 1918.

83rd. Field Company. R.E.

Officer Commanding.		
Major. L.E. HOPKINS.	July. 1915.	August. 1916.
Capt. J.A.C. PENNYCUICK. D.S.O.	August. 1916.	October. 1916.
A/Major. I.W. MASSIE. M.C.	November. 1916.	October. 1918.
A/Major. T.W.R. HAYCRAFT.	October. 1918.	January. 1919.
A/Capt. R.H. HODGSON.	March. 1919.	

84th Field Company. R.E.

Major. H.S. CHRISTIE.	September. 1914.	January. 1916.
Capt. P.G. HUDDLESTON.	January. 1916.	March. 1916.
Major. M.A.H. SCOTT. M.C.	March. 1916.	June. 1917.
A/Major. P.G. NORMAN. M.C.	June. 1917.	October. 1918.
A/Major. W.A.R. BOURNE. M.C.	November. 1918.	

96th Field Company. R.E.

Major. A.C. SCOTT.	October. 1914.	November. 1915.
Major. P.F. STORY. D.S.O.	November. 1915.	April. 1918.
A/Major. E.B. HUGH-JONES. M.C.	April. 1918	

20th Div. Signal Coy. R.E.

Major. F.J.M. STRATTON. D.S.O.	November. 1914	June. 1917.
Major. A.G. BRACE. M.C.	June. 1917.	

10/3/19.

E.M. Newell
Lieut-Colonel. R.E.
C.R.E. 20th Division.

HONOURS & AWARDS

(41)

No.	Rank	Name	Date	Remarks
48838	Sgt	Perrin L. A.	6.11.15	Awarded Croix de Guerre
48835	Cpl	Bee W.		D.C.M
44392	Sgt	Molloy	15.6.16	Mentd. in Despt.
52538	L/Cpl	Barber H	22.10.16	Awarded M.M.
44392	Sgt	Molloy	27.10.16	" Do
48829	A/Sgt	Pepall	27.10.16	" Do
46671	Cpl	Sinclair N	9.2.17	Medaille Militaire
48835	Sgt	Bee W.	25.4.17	Military Medal
49772	Cpl	Hamilton J.	-"-	Do Do
48840	L/Cpl	Reed	-"-	Do Do
46200	2/Cpl	Wilson C.	18.5.17	Mentd. in Despt.
46665	L/Cpl	Thompson C.	4.9.17	Awarded M.M.
61070	Driver	Baker	22.9.17	Do Do
48744	2/Cpl	Stokes G.	3.10.17	Do Do
46205	Cpl	Joyce J.	22.4.18	Do Do
50957	2/Cpl	Gibson C.	22.4.18	Do Do
61951	L/Cpl	Webster J.	15.8.18	Do Do
50958	Sgt	Thompson G.		Do Do
61873	2/Cpl	Morgan R. W.	25.2.19	Do Do

"Officers"

Rank	Name	Date	Remarks
Lieut	J. G. Schon		M.C.
2/Lieut	H.Y.V. Jackson		M.C.
Lieut	R.A. Bagnold	18.5.17	Mentd. in Despt.
Lieut	T.A. Smith	"	Do Do
Lieut	F.H. Poole	29.4.18	awarded M.C.
Major	J.W. Massie M.C.	8.5.18	-"- bar to M.C.

N.C.O.'s & MEN. KILLED

No.	Rank	Name	Date KILLED.	Remarks
49941	Sapr	Fisher L. A.	14.9.15	(Died of wounds)
49178	"	Hanks A. E.	15.9.15	
48751	"	Bragg H.	25.9.15	
61890	"	James J. D.	25.9.15	
97255	L/Corpl.	Polglass A.	25.9.15	
49199	Sapper	Hall W. E.	25.9.15	
63151	"	Harvey J.	9.10.15	
57370	"	Ellett H.	12.11.15	
49198	"	Borthwick R.		
48253	L/Corpl.	Macdonald R.	22.2.16	
59346	Sapper	Caine T.	22.2.16	
43315	"	Wallace J.		
49175	"	Melluish E.	22.2.16	
61863	"	Askew L.	2.7.16	(Died of Wounds)
48760	Pioneer	Hicks F. V.	2.7.16	
66609	Sapr	Smith A. J.	29.8.16	
48825	"	Gatrell W.	29.8.16	
43314	A/Sgt.	Yuille W.	7.10.16	
145715	Sapper	Sheriff W.	7.10.16	
59332	"	Muckleston H.	7.10.16	
48841	"	Howard A. E.	9.10.16	
49196	"	Hansom J. J.	9.10.16	
48824	"	Hinton O.	27.10.16	(Died of Wounds)
61072	Driver	Shepherd T.	11.11.16	(Drowned)
65822	Sapper	Stacey L.	4.4.17	
131296	"	Woodall A.	4.4.17	
134681	"	Ross W.	12.4.17	(Died of Wounds)
121004	"	Holmes H. B.	4.5.17	
44849	"	Grew H.	31.5.17	(Died of Wounds)
153701	"	Denton U.	12.8.17	
217628	"	Wood A.	12.8.17	
212349	"	Thomas H.	11.9.17	
420133	"	Lauchlan J.	11.9.17	
467867	"	Robson W.	11.9.17	
44847	"	Kerr K.	11.9.17	
105164	Driver	Hazledine J.	20.9.17	(Died of Wounds)
141048	L/Corpl.	Damp H.	15.9.17	
61071	Driver	Maddams E.	18.9.17	(Died of Wounds)
48246	Sapper	Borthwick J.	3.11.17	
59371	"	Shaw A.	30.11.17	
23267	"	Warrener H. T.	23.3.18	
46139	"	Sharpe W.	23.3.18	

N.C.O.'s & MEN "Killed"

No.	Rank	Name	Date when Killed	Remarks
211772	L/Corpl.	Ashford	24.3.18	(Believed killed)
180086	Sapr.	Coles. C.	25.3.18	(Died of Wounds)
48829	Sgt	Pepall	24.3.18	(Died of Wounds)
402396	L/Corpl.	Fletcher	13.5.18	
164741	Sapper	Wetherill	13.5.18	

"Officers"

	Rank	Name	Date	Remarks
	Lieut	Jervis R.N.	5.1.16	
	2/Lieut	Mitchell P.J.	17.8.17	(Died of Wounds)
	Lieut	Lee L.B.	30.11.17	

1st May – Aug. trench duties in LENS Sector
Aug – 6th Oct trench work at VIMY
(During these periods assistance was frequently
given to Infantry Battalions in making raids)

On taking over Command of Coy on Nov. 17th 1918 I found Capt J.E. Bird. R.E. had been in temporary command for about a month – he became my 2nd in Command, +Lieut f. E.A Presnell RE Senior Subaltern, with +Lieuts f. Brown, E. f. Hoar & D. Campion completing the Coy's officers.
Lieut Presnell's & Lieut Hoar's work & powers of organisation have always been of a very high standard.
+Lieut Brown & Campion with their sections went forward to VILLERS-SIRE-NICHOLE immediately following the Armistice & carried out works in connection with the erection of bridges making good of roads destroyed by land mines in a most efficient & rapid way
+Lieut P. TRIPLETE R.E. joined the Coy after the Armistice.
The work of the following N.C.O.s has at all times been of an excellent character
Sergt OLDALE. E. B. (now C.S.M.) } Section Sergeants
  "   TAYLOR . W.
Staff Farrier Sergt. RATHBONE . J. } Mounted Section
Sergt. ALLISON . R. Mounted Sergt.
Corporal & DIXON . H.

Lieut A. E. Marshall. RASC.

I attach herewith notes in connection with the Battle History of this Coy; the task has not been an easy one as there have been such constant changes of Command. I trust however that they may be of some guidance in your rather arduous job.

I should very much like the names of Officers & E.O's I have mentioned, during my period of Command, to be mentioned in the History if possible as they have received no awards.

W. A. R. Bourne
Major. RE.
OC. 84th Field Coy. RE.

12-3-19.

Notes on History of 86th Field Co RE

Formed at Chatham about Sept 1st/14. Major H.S. Christie RE. OC
March to Aldershot. Sept.
— Woking. early in Dec/14
Officers Major H.S. Christie Capt P.G. Huddleston ii Lts I.W. Massie
J.C.L. Train. P.S. Moorman & G.W. Rower.

Pontooning Wargrave on Thames Jany & Feby/15
Larkhill March 25 to July 22nd/15
Havre 23.7.15. Merris & Armentieres Aug/15
under instruction in the line by 8th Div. at Bois Grenier.
Laventie sector Oct to Dec/15.
Rest Jany/16. Salient from Feby 10th/16 to
about April 10th/16. From Canal near BOESINGHE to
"D22" N.E. of YPRES. Company constructed 1100ⁿ of
semi-breastwork trench in No Mans Land from
"S32" to the right - about 500 men employed nightly from Res Bde.

April 1 week spent at Calais in rest. then
relieved guards Div on right Div front of 1x Corps E of
YPRES. Coy constructed CAVAN trench on the left of
Wieltje. also rebuilt BOND Street
June 2 Raids in front of Railway Wood.
① Lt Earl & party no results
② Lt H.S. Morrisby & party, brought back information
   & prisoners also destroyed MG emplac.
August/16 in line opposite SERRE, employed on
recovering front line destroyed on July 1st
End of August & 1st & 2nd September constructed 'pid.' assembly
trenches in front of Guillemont which according to Brig Gen
Shute. to Bg C 59th Bde made it possible to take G on
Sept 3rd
Oct 1st & Oct 7th employed with 61st Bde on
GUEDECOURT front when 61st was the only Bde in
4th Army to get any objectives. Coy personally congratulated
by B.G.C. 61st Bde, G.O.C. 20th Div & G.O.C. XIV Corps
(Earl Cavan).
Rest at DAOURS for about 6 weeks then in
line MORVAL sector, usual trench work.
SAILLY - SAILLISEL. Jany & Feby & March/17 ditto
March & April. during Huns retreat, removed Booby traps etc
& worked on water supply in TRANSLOY area reconstructed
the road between ROCQUINY & Bapaume — S. Saillisel Road.
then usual trench war in & around Havrincourt Wood.
April May & June/17. in Lagnicourt & Noreuil
Sectors, usual trench work.

July/17. Rest. Built large concrete swimming bath on YSER R. N.W. of PROVEN.

Aug Built plank road Canal Bank (Bridge 6W) through No Mans Land to HUDDLESTONE Road later built mule track from point on PILCKEM - YPRES Road to S of IRON CROSS to join PILCKEM - LANGEMARCK Road

Sept 16/17. Div captured LANGEMARCK. Co constr bridges STEENBEEK R. E of PILCKEM. Lt E.C. Delamain R.E. awarded MC for this.

Oct/17. in line E of VILLERS GUISLAIN. usual trench work.

Nov./17. Co constructed numerous camouflaged shelters & bivouacs for battle on 20th Nov. 1 Bn camp constructed on open field E of HEUDECOURT which was invisible from the air.

Nov 20. Coy put 23 Artillery bridges over trenches & maintained them (No 3 Section under Lt. Martyn R.E). rear of Coy on strong points.

Nov 22 - 29. Consolidating position SE of MASNIERES.

Nov 30 - Dec 5. Employed as Infy in Bosch Counter attack

Dec 12 (about) to Jany 11th rear line defences on WYCHAETE Ridge E of the BLUFF.

Jany & Feby trench work in GHELUVELT sector.

March Rear Line defences on SOMME from HAM to VOYENNES. 700 Italians attached.

March 21st - till March 27th attached 61st Bde & used as Infantry.

March 27 - April 1st digging trench lines under C.R.E. from LE QUESNEL to DOMART.

Rest till May 1st

Officer Casualties.

Lt C.A. CURRIE. R.E.   Killed   Dec/15.
Capt P.G. HUDDLESTON -   - March/16
" Lt.? MARTYN   -   - Nov. /17

Awards.
Major M A H Scott R.E -   MC & one or 2 mentions
Lt J W Massie   MC
Lt CA CURRIE   Mention
 - R H Warde   M.C.
 - H E Hill   M.C.
 - J.C. Bird   Medaille Agricole.
 - E.C. Delamain   MC
 - EA Earl   Mention
 - H.S. Macristy   M.C.
Major Self. P.G NORMAN   MC & 2 mentions
O/c Major W.C.R. Bourne   M.C.   2.1.19

Major H.S. Christie R.E. 1.9.14 to 27.1.16
Capt P.G. Huddleston   27.1.16 - 25.3.16
Major M A H Scott   25.3.16 - 16.6.17
" Self. P G NORMAN   16.6.17 - 21.10.18.   Major W.C.R Bourne 1/11/18 - todate

Wounded (42)

824 Field Co RE

Reg'n No	Rank	Name		Date
44522	L Corpl	Davidson J.A. *	Wounded (at duty)	2-9-15
43739	Sergt	Thomas J.A.	Wounded	20-9-15
44886	L Corpl	Dixson J.	"	21-9-15
45296	Sapr	Dickie W.	" (at duty)	29-10-15
44815	L Corpl	Pratt J.H.	"	6-11-15
16325	Sapr	Curby J.R.	"	30-11-15
	Lieut	P.G. Norman RE *	"	2-12-15
45288	Sapr	Elliott W.	" (at duty)	8-12-15
59420	"	Guest S.	"	16-12-15
52136	L Corpl	Edworthy W.	"	28-12-15
44615	Sapr	Popham C.	"	28-12-15
53932	Driver	Houlton E.	" (at duty)	31-12-15
17268	Sapper	McFarlane J.	"	4-1-16
92658	"	Milliard J. *	"	5-1-16
44634	"	Whittall R.	" (at duty)	15-2-16
134677	"	Benton E.	"	22-2-16
45059	Corpl	McKay A.	"	2-3-16
103365	Sapr	McEvoy P.	"	8-3-16
44888	Sergt	Harvey V.D.	"	19-3-16
49016	"	Kerley H. *	" (at duty)	19-3-16
59347	Sapr	Driscoll W.	" (at duty)	19-3-16
61894		McMillan W. *	" (at duty)	20-3-16
	Lieut	P.G. Norman *	" (at duty)	23-3-16
53920	L Corpl	Furness A.	"	1-4-16
53703	Driver	Hearne D.	"	1-4-16
49016	Sergt	Kerley H. *	"	6-4-16
45295	Sapr	Adam J.	"	6-4-16
44854	"	Stokes G.	"	6-4-16
57256	"	Pearce J.A.	"	9-4-16
61754	"	McTaggart D. *	" (at duty)	3-6-16
45088	Corpl	Taylor W.P.	"	8-6-16
	2 Lieut	E.A. Earl *	"	13-6-16
43732	Sapr	Cornall R.	"	13-6-16
40701	Corpl	Sircombe J.C. *	" (at duty)	13-6-16
	Lieut	H.S. Manisty	"	26-6-16
44829	Sapr	Edmonds A.	"	26-6-16
59477	"	Kennell J.W.	"	27-6-16
134844	"	Munro W.J.	" (at duty)	27-6-16
43722	"	Killey A.	"	29-6-16

Regtl No.	Rank	Name	Casualty	Date
48943	Sapper	Hinks. T. *	Wounded	2-7-16
134703	"	Blackman. J.J.B	" (at duty)	2-8-16
44645	Corpl	Stevenson. J *	" (at duty)	25-8-16
	2/Lieut	E. A. Glover	"	26-8-16
45339	2/Corpl	Vernon. G.A *	"	27-8-16
61897	L/Corpl	Clegg. H. *	"	31-8-16
44831	2/Corpl	Crolly. J	"	3-9-16
45341	Sapper	Martin. W.C.	"	3-9-16
44634	"	Whittle. R.	"	3-9-16
59132	"	Watkinson. J	"	3-9-16
58299	"	Hillary. R.J	"	3-9-16
44855	"	Earley. W	"	3-9-16
44816	"	Murrell. W *	"	3-9-16
44521	Sergt	Rust. A.	" (at duty)	3-9-16
45075	C.S.M.	Green. S.	" (at duty)	3-9-16
113735	Sapper	Eaves. W.	" (at duty)	3-9-16
59345	"	Bosher. A. *	" (at duty)	3-9-16
61992	"	Morris. C.H	"	4-9-16
61898	"	Doidge. W.J	"	4-9-16
	2/Lieut	W.A.A. Morris	"	5-9-16
44853	Sapr	Berry. R *	"	16-9-16
61754	"	McTaggart. D *	"	16-9-16
45260	2/Cpl	Hillman. J *	" (Shell shock)	16-9-16
61892	L/Corpl	Seymour. M	"	18-9-16
44582	L/Corpl	Pent. J.W. *	"	18-9-16
61894	Sapr	McMillan. W *	"	1-4-16
44822	Corpl	Davidson. J.A *	" (at duty)	18-9-16
45314	"	Perkins. A.B.	"	1-10-16
40568	Sapr	Wylie. J	"	1-10-16
51597	"	Hight. J	"	1-10-16
44619	"	Harrison. W.J	"	1-10-16
44641	"	Nicol. A.C	"	1-10-16
95406	"	Cook. R.	" (at duty)	1-10-16
40252	"	Nason. W	"	18-9-16
44889	Sergt	Nevitt. J.B.	"	7-10-16
63180	Sapr	Warburton. G.	"	7-10-16
40304	"	Bolt. W.E.	"	7-10-16
45310	"	McDonald. D.	" (at Duty)	7-10-16
45284	L/Corpl	Davies.	"	7-10-16
105350	Sapper	Tyson. R.E.	"	24-2-17
37392	"	Davies. R.	"	27-2-17

3

REG.Tl N°	RANK	NAME	CASUALTY	DATE
45297	2nd Corpl	Millar J.	Wounded	1-4-17
26759	"	Lane G.	"	8-6-17
45342	Sapper	Crewe A.	" (at duty)	8-6-17
58912	"	Tinsley E.A.	"	9-6-17
45345	"	Aggett N.B.	"	8-8-17
44883	"	Berry A.	"	10-8-17
146678	"	Heath J.B.	"	10-8-17
45058	L/Corpl	Montgomery R.	"	10-8-17
61599	Sapper	McMillan G.A.	"	10-8-17
146754	"	Holt J.E.	"	10-8-17
61990	Corpl.	Martin A.	"	10-8-17
45255	Sapper	Ingram R.	"	10-8-17
166217	"	Hooking M.	"	10-8-17
166352	"	Bellis H.C.	"	10-8-17
44882	L/Corpl	Peart J.D.	"	10-8-17
	2/Lieut	S.S. Spencer R.E.	"	11-8-17
	"	J. Belloc R.E.	"	11-8-17
43735	Sapper	Keatley G.L.	"	13-8-17
145878	"	Fulford M.	" (at Duty)	13-8-17
45342	"	Crewe A.	"	14-8-17
164446	"	Hester C.	"	14-8-17
93510	"	Kelly A.	"	14-8-17
45952	"	Bray J.	" (at duty)	14-8-17
140467	"	Johnstone R.S.	"	16-8-17
69345	Corpl	Koster A.	"	16-8-17
61951	L/Corpl	Smith R.	"	16-8-17
400313	Sapper	Walkinshaw J.	"	16-8-17
400505	"	Brown H.	"	14-8-17
89333	"	Morgan E.	" (at duty)	16-8-17
44816	"	Murrell M.	" (at duty)	16-8-17
496946	"	Desborough R.G.	" (at duty)	16-8-17
40701	Corpl	Sircombe S.C.	"	11-9-17
131100	Sapper	Walls J.	"	11-9-17
154390	"	Nelson M.	"	15-9-17
	2/Lieut	E.A. Earl R.E.	" (at duty)	21-9-17
63983	Sapper	Racher E.	"	21-9-17
153995	"	Batchelor D.	"	21-9-17
97335	"	Fisher J.	"	21-9-17
416246	"	Hollingworth E.	"	21-9-17
45313	"	Rodgers C.A.	"	21-9-17
36159	Sergt	Clapp H.	"	21-9-17
90477	Dr	Brown G.T.	"	24-9-17
80241	"	Wilson F.C.	"	24-9-17

Regt^l No	Rank	Name	Casualty	Date
80235	L/Corpl	Hayes. J.	Wounded	24-9-17
	Capt	G. A. Kohl R.E.	"	27-9-17
26759	Corpl	Lane. G. *	"	28-11-17
164990	Sapr	Arnold. W.E.	"	28-11-17
151107	"	Quail. J.W.	"	28-11-17
61109	Driver	Taylor. W.	"	28-11-17
44606	Sapr	Jones. P.	"	29-11-17
45307	"	Shields. J.	"	29-11-17
44617	"	Green. H.R.	" (at duty)	30-11-17
80237	Driver	Edmead. G.J.B.	"	30-11-17
159413	L/Corpl	Baldwin. W.G.	"	30-11-17
408114	Sapper	Murray. W.S.	"	30-11-17
166697	"	Bell. D.A.	"	2-12-17
184372	"	Marrett. G. *	"	2-12-17
402457	"	Fleming. E.	" (Gas)	3-1-18
89265	"	Cox. J.	" (Gas)	3-1-18
155264	"	Kyle. G.	" (Gas)	3-1-18
	Lieut	G.W. Porter	" (Gas)	4-1-18
92658	Sapr	Millward. J. *	" (at duty)	11-1-18
	Lieut	Hill. A.E.	"	16-1-18
44884	Sapr	Carver. W.	"	22-1-18
101518	Corpl	Hazlewood. W.	"	22-1-18
61896	L/Corpl	Wilson. J.	"	10-2-18
145260	Corpl	Hillman. H. *	"	10-2-18
52135	Driver	Alston	"	23-3-18
48943	L/Corpl	Hinks. J. *	"	24-3-18
120883	Sapr	Green. K.	Wounded & Missing	24-3-18
30938	"	Lamb. G.	Wounded	24-3-18
159754	"	Smith. C.	Wounded & Missing	24-3-18
	Lieut	G. Pitt R.E.	Wounded	24-3-18
45326	Sapr	Waller. C. *	"	24-3-18
140329	"	Girvan. R.	" (at duty)	24-3-18
508226	"	Bendall. M.	"	24-3-18
177313	"	Barrow. R.	"	24-3-18
540653	"	Marchant. S.	"	24-3-18
154390	"	Nelson. M. *	"	24-3-18
410418	"	Young. L.	"	24-3-18
143734	Corpl	Ross. G.	Wounded & Missing	26-3-18
103604	Sergt	Branston. A.	"	26-3-18
	Lieut	Peters R.E.	" (Gas)	21-3-18

5

Regtl No	Rank	Name	Casualty	Date
251734	Sapr	Whitchurch D.L	Wounded (at duty)	9-5-18
58193	"	Fairbairn G.	Wounded	11-4-18
	Lieut	J. W. Leslie R.E.	" (Gas)	19-5-18
552757	Sapper	Reeves	" (Gas)	22-5-18
230882	"	Sparkes H.	" (Gas)	29-5-18
91053	Driver	Stokeley G.	" (Gas)	2-6-18
446570	Sapr	Owen J	" (Gas)	2-6-18
508081	"	Sandilands	"	29-3-18
448822	Sergt	Davidson A.J. *	"	26-3-18
546743	Sapr	Poulton L	"	19-6-18
440544	"	Cockcroft	" (Gas)	2-7-18
45326	"	Waller C *	" (Gas)	2-7-18
396456	"	Moran J	" (Gas)	2-7-18
166673	"	Wiles A	"	2-7-18
440546	L/Corpl	Allman G	"	2-7-18
115936	Sapper	Goodman E	"	2-7-18
476252	"	Nettleship A	"	2-7-18
61887	T/Corpl	Klegg H *	"	2-7-18
422154	Sapr	Robertson A.	"	2-7-18
45294	"	Halliday J.	"	2-7-18
45308	"	McAllister J	"	2-7-18
95181	"	Gill F.	"	2-7-18
69615	T/Corpl	Rochester S	"	3-7-18
45260	"	Allman A *	"	1-7-18
42521	Driver	Parkinson A	"	1-7-18
153893	L/Corpl	Pearce J	"	1-7-18
22762	Sapper	Lewis J A	"	1-7-18
61746	"	Watkins W	"	1-7-18
213674	"	Berry W	"	1-7-18
496946	"	Desborough A *	"	1-7-18
486928	Driver	Brady G	"	1-7-18
44816	Sapr	Murrell W *	"	1-7-18
474131	"	Newson W	"	1-7-18
489142	"	Annesley C	"	1-7-18
145878	"	Fulford W *	"	1-7-18
154141	"	Halyter F	"	1-7-18
152748	Driver	Whitcombe A		1-7-18
422057	Sapr	Smith W.J		1-7-18

6

Regt'l No	Rank	Name	Casualty	Date
458952	Sapr	Bray J. *	Wounded (Gas)	1-7-18
153856	"	Goldstein S.	" "	6-7-18
108787	"	Aitchen J.	" "	6-7-18
290045	"	Alcock J.	" "	6-7-18
104328	"	Pringle A.	" "	6-7-18
517534	"	McTaggart D. *	" "	6-7-18
45339	L Corpl	Vernon G. *	" "	6-7-18
114645	Sergt	Stevenson J. *	Wounded (Gas)	22-7-18
231981	Sapr	Hawkins E.	Wounded (at duty)	23-7-18
45569	"	Thomson R.J.	" "	23-7-18
244216	"	Trickett A.	" "	31-7-18
104372	"	Smart R.	" "	7-8-18
490204	L Corpl	Evans A.	" "	26-9-18
164829	"	Innes J.	" "	27-9-18
107180	Pion	Rock E.	" "	27-9-18

* Denotes Offrs & ORs wounded more than once

Killed, Missing and Died of Wounds.

Reg'tl No	Rank	Name	Casualty	Date
45261	Sapper	Hereford A.	Killed in Action	28-10-15
45280	Pioneer	Chanler J	" "	28-10-15
44614	Sapper	Klower P.	" "	31-10-15
	Lieut	C.A. Currie R.E.	" "	18-12-15
59372	Sapper	Taylor W.P	" "	30-12-15
80232	Driver	Elder D.	" "	22-2-16
	Capt	S.G. Huddleston		25-3-16
44836	Sapper	Hunt A.	" "	6-4-16
18342	"	Mullee J.	" "	14-4-16
45274	"	Rhodes C.D	" "	26-6-16
44881	Corpl	Pearson A.	" "	3-9-16
59340	L/Corpl	Brown A.J	" "	18-9-16
140125	Sapper	Richardson G.H.	" "	18-9-16
61979	"	Stuart A.S	" "	18-9-16
51601	"	Craddock W.	Missing	2-10-16
56832	"	Cowell J.W.	"	2-10-16
44613	"	Toplam A.	Killed in action	4-10-16
44829	"	Edmonds A.	Died of Wounds	
45301	L/Corpl	Craig A.H	Killed in action	26-5-17
108681	Sapper	Curran J.	" "	14-9-17
	Lieut	F.H. Martin R.E	" "	24-11-17
61105	Driver	Burch W.J	" "	25-11-17
61109	"	Taylor W.	Died of wounds	28-11-17
524478	Sapper	Warner G	Killed in action	2-12-17
98510	"	Kelly A.	Died of wounds	30-8-17
408114	"	Murray W.S	" "	17-12-17
184372	"	Marrett G	" "	10-2-18
20869	L/Corpl	Gower G	Killed in action	24-3-18
398872	Sapper	Jones D.	Missing	26-3-18
402256	"	Strathdee W.	"	26-3-18
37437	"	Wicklam A	"	26-3-18
185696	"	Cousins A.W	"	26-3-18
414774	"	Develin A	"	26-3-18
143534	"	Dodgson W.	"	26-3-18
43735	"	Keatley G	"	26-3-18
224305	"	John D.		26-3-18
45259	Corpl	Buckingham G	Killed in action	22-5-18
457548	Sapper	Barber A.G	Died of Wounds	23-5-18
494257	"	Cooper W.	Killed in action	7-8-18
215885	"	Powell A.E.	" "	27-9-18

84 Field Company R.E. — Honours and Awards

Regt No	Rank	Name	Honours & Awards	Date
	Lieut	J.W. Massie	Awarded M.C.	3-1-16
44886	L/Corpl	Dixon F.	Mentioned	3-1-16
44888	Sergt	Harvey V.D.	Awarded D.C.M.	14-1-16
	Lieut	C.A. Currie	Mentioned	3-1-16
	Lieut	R.A. Warde	do	15-6-16
49016	Sergt	Kerley A.	do	15-6-16
	Lieut	A.T. Manisty	Awarded M.C.	2-7-16
45059	Sergt	McKay A.	" M.M.	2-7-16
44822	Corpl	Davidson J.A.	" "	27-9-16
44869	Sergt	Nevitt J.B.	Div. mentioned	26-9-16
44611	Corpl	McLiesh D.	do do	26-9-16
44895	L/Corpl	Handley C.	Awarded M.M.	26-10-16
43734	Corpl	Ross G.	do do	19-10-16
59345	L/Corpl	Bosher A.	do do	19-10-16
44821	Sergt	Rust A.G.	do do	27-10-16
49016		Kerley A.	do do	27-10-16
	Major	M.A.R. Scott	do M.C.	1-1-17
	Lieut	R.A. Warde	do M.C.	15-1-17
		H.E. Hill	Mentioned	2-1-17
	Major	P.G. Norman	Awarded M.C.	7-6-17
53164	L/Corpl	Keech	do M.M.	25-8-17
61896	Sapper	Wilson J.	do M.M.	25-8-17
45075	C.S.M.	Green J.	Mentioned	18-5-17
44617	Sapper	Green K.R.	Mentioned	18-5-17
	1 Lieut	E.C. Delamain	Awarded M.C.	31-8-17
	1 Lieut	J.E. Bird	Awarded Medal Ajudicle	6-10-17
	Major	P.G. Norman	Mentioned	17-12-17
60164	Corpl	Horsfall J.	Mentioned	17-12-17
53159	Corpl	Spreadbury F.	Awarded M.M.	31-12-17
40701	Corpl	Sircombe S.C.	Div Mentioned	
40701		Sircombe S.C.	Awarded D.C.M.	1-1-18
	Major	P.G. Norman	Mentioned	21-2-18
45259	Corpl	Buckingham G.S.	Awarded D.C.M.	6-6-18
244216	Sapper	Trickitt A.	" M.M.	21-8-18
44645	Sergt	Stevenson J.	" M.M.	25-2-19
45297	Corpl	Millar J.	" D.C.M.	2-1-19
94810	Sergt	Kent W.E.	Mentioned	8-11-18
140528	L/Corpl	Girvan R.	do	8-11-18
	Major	W.A.R. Bourne	Awarded M.C.	3-1-19

NOTES FOR HISTORY OF 96th FIELD COY. R.E.

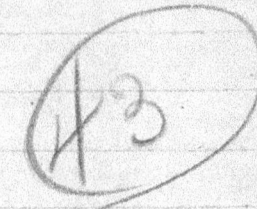

The Company started its career at CHATHAM in October 1914, and was at first part of the 26th Division, but when the number of Field Companies per Division was increased to three, it joined the 20th Division, in training at LARK HILL on SALISBURY PLAIN in May 1915.

The Company first saw Active Service on the LAVENTIE FRONT, where in three and a half months it dug over 4100 yards of new communication trenches, thickened the parapet to 15 feet along the Front of the 59th Infantry Brigade, with whom the Company has worked for the last 4½ years; the whole of the Front Line was rebuilt, and the existing Strong points and Reserve Line completed. The first concrete machine-gun emplacement made by the Division was put in by the 96th Field Company in this area, to protect the RED LAMP SALIENT, which the Company later eliminated by building a sandbag breastwork 290 yards long, this contained over 10,000 sandbags which were laid in one night.

The YPRES SALIENT in 1916 the Company was employed in reclaiming the Front-line system and improving communications. A very large number of framed machine-gun emplacements with concrete head-cover were made, including a double one in FOCH FARM; provision for storing Gas-cylinders was made in the Front line. An average of 4 tons of R.E. material was taken up the line from the Company workshops and Dumps each night.

On the SOMME, in the Autumn of 1916, after preparing dumps of material and digging 'jumping-off' trenches for the attack on GUILLEMONT, 2 Sections went over with the attacking Infantry and consolidated the objective, and in the 3 following nights, dug and wired a new Front line of posts.

During the German retirement in the Spring of 1917, the Company was mostly employed on removing mines and booby traps, opening up water supply and wiring the new line after each jump forward.

In the FLANDERS attack 1917 the construction of plank roads, duckboard tracks and light railways composed of the majority of the work. Strong points were also made immediately after each attack and for these large battle-dumps of material were made as far forward as possible before the attack.

At CAMBRAI in November 1917, the line reached by the 59th Infantry Brigade was wired. After the German counter-attack the Company manned a line of defence along RILEY AVENUE and FUSILIER RESERVE LINE in front of Brigade Headquarters.

During the retreat in March 1918, six bridges across the SOMME RIVER were blown up by the Company and five more across the Canal were prepared for demolition; eight distinct lines of defence were dug by the Company, the first some

3 miles east of NESLE and the last 1½ miles West of DOMART-SUR-LA-LUCE; on each occasion every man dug a treble task, 15 feet of 3 by 3 trench.

The period spent in the LENS SECTOR provided a larger variety of work than had ever been met with before. Camps, baths, bomb screens, and rifle ranges in the area of the Transport Lines, road-bridges and screens, new defence lines, concrete pill-boxes, concrete observation posts, innumerable dugouts and shelters, the construction of Light Railways to the outpost line for the discharge of Gas, and demolition work in connection with raids on enemy dugouts were carried out during the course of the Summer.

E. F. Hugh-Jones

MAJOR, R.E.
O.C. 96th FIELD COY. R.E.

Names of Commanding Officers of 96 Field Coy. R.E.

Major A.C. Scott. RE. from 15th Oct. 1914 to 20th Novr. 1915
Major P.F. Story. D.S.O. RE. " 21st Novr. 1915 to 16th April 1918.
Major E.B. Hugh-Jones M.C. RE. – 17th April 1918 to Present time

96th FIELD COMPANY R.E.

Nominal Roll of Officers, N.C.O.s and Men, Killed in Action, or Died of Wounds.

Number	Rank	Name	Casualty	Date	Place
	Lieut	G.C. Grant	Died of Wounds	14-10-1915	Laventie
	"	A.M.M. Bascombe-Harrison	"	27-10-1915	"
	"	R.W. Formby	Killed	16-2-1917	Lesboeufs
	2nd Lieut	J.H. Best	"	25-6-1916	Ypres
	"	A.T. Andrews	"	25-6-1916	"
	"	G. Mitchell	Died of Wounds	17-8-1917	Pilkem Ridge Ypres
48542	Sergt	T. Wray	Killed	25-6-1916	Ypres
48703	Farr Sgt	J. Wansbrough	"	27-9-1917	"
45928	Corpl	P. Morrison	Died of Wounds	25-3-1918	Gruny
49661	2nd Corpl	H. Kitchener M.M.	Killed	5-10-1916	Ginchy Ridge
56967	L/Cpl	F.J. Dyke	"	9-10-1915	Laventie
49567	"	W. Hibbert	"	3-9-1916	Guillemont
63456	"	D.H. Smith	"	"	"
50057	"	W. Dickenson	"	"	"
154279	"	F. Moorhouse	"	3-12-1917	Villers-Plouich
50041	Sapper	W. Jackson	"	23-9-1915	Laventie
50068	"	G. Culling	"	20-3-1916	Ypres
46365	"	W. Purcell	"	25-6-1916	"
100780	"	W. Baker	"	3-9-1916	Guillemont
63452	"	H. Taylor	"	"	"
49561	"	H. Vincent	"	"	"
48457	"	J.W. Christon	Died of Wounds	"	"
65712	"	R. Warden	"	25-5-1917	Vaulx
159962	"	F. Moss	Killed	21-11-1917	Rue de Vignes Nr Cambrai
146766	"	N. Saunders	Died of Wounds	"	"
45970	"	G. Heath	"	13-1-1918	Gheluvelt
167724	"	B. Stead	Killed	16-8-1918	Lens Sector
45842	Pioneer	C. Chapman	Died of Wounds	5-8-1915	Laventie
107236	"	J. Lockett	"	1-12-1917	Villers-Plouich
807-25	Driver	H. Smith	Killed	23-9-1915	Laventie
80736	"	H.J. England	Died of Wounds	30-11-1917	La Vacquerie

6 Officers and 96 other Ranks have been WOUNDED

LIST OF OFFICERS, W.O's, N.C.O's & MEN WHO HAVE RECEIVED HONOURS AND AWARDS WITH 96th FIELD Coy. RE

No	RANK	NAME	AWARD	REMARKS
	MAJOR	P.F. STORY	D.S.O.	
	MAJOR	E.B. HUGH-JONES	M.C.	
	CAPT.	R.H. WARDE	M.C.	
	CAPT.	R.M.F. HUDDART	M.C.	
	LIEUT.	L.L. WILLIAMS	M.C.	
	LIEUT.	D. LANG	M.C.	
47748	C.S.M.	A. BALL	M.S.M.	
48712	Sergt	W. MARTIN	M.M.	
45921	"	J. RITSON	M.M.	
—	Corpl	A. GIBSON	M.M.	
49661	L/Corpl	H. KITCHENER	M.M.	
58652	L/Corpl	H. FRICKER	M.S.M.	
50053	Sapper	J. ALLEN	D.C.M.	
159986	Sapper	V. HOSKINS	M.M.	
	Sapper	H. JOHNSON	D.C.M.	
48697	Sapper	W. ROYAL	M.M.	
80723	Driver	F.G. ADAMS	M.M.	
63486	Sergt	J.B. MONAGHAN	}	Mentioned in
49568	"	E. BAXTER	}	Despatches.
50075	Corpl	W. McILROY	}	Mentioned in FIFTH ARMY
45692	2/Corpl	G.H. POOLE	}	ROUTINE ORDER FOR
143814	Sapper	C.J. BURGOYNE	}	GALLANT CONDUCT on
62160	"	F. PARRINGTON	}	24-7-17

=SUMMARY=

| D.S.O's | 1 | D.C.M's | 2 | M.M. | 7 |
| M.C's | 5 | M.S.M's | 2 | Mentions | 2 |

Postal Section
Offices.

Railhead A.P.O.	Connecting link between Div. & L. of C.
Div HQ. F.P.O.	For Divnl HQ Unit
Train F.P.O	For Divnl Artillery
3 Bgde F.P.Os	One for each Infantry Brigade.

Arrival & Despatch of Mails

Special Express Mails are received and delivered daily to Divnl HQ & Infantry Bgde H.Q. These are conveyed from the Base by Postal lorries and contain correspondence posted in Eng. two to three days previous to the delivery at the respective HQs. Other mails arrive with supplies at the Divnl Railhead, and are sorted at the Railhead A.P.O for distribution by Postal lorries at the Divisional Field P.Os. There they are handed over to the Post Orderlies of Units, who have already handed in the postings ~~of their respective units~~ to be sorted and despatched to the Railhead P.O by the returning lorry. At the Railhead P.O these are re-sorted into bags for London; the main provincial centres of England and Army P.O Depots in the B.E.F. All letters for Eng. are forwarded by Postal lorry to the Base and loaded on the boat the day after posting at any Field P.O. in the Division.

The average number of Bags dealt with daily at the Railhead P.O. is 150

Average No. of Regt. letters daily 200

During Xmas pressure these numbers are more than trebled.

Since the commencement of the sale of War Saving Certificates in the BEF Officers NCOs & men of the Division have purchased more than 10,000 through L.P.O.

Through the sale of Postal Orders an average of 10,000 francs each week is handed over to the Field Cashier. In congested areas the Railhead P.O. alone has handed to the Field Cashier as much as 16,000 fcs in one week.

During the time the Division has been in the BEF with the exception of the strenuous time in March mails have been delivered without fail on the day of its arrival at Railhead and all letters for England posted at the L.P.O. have been forwarded on the date of posting. In the March battle only Express & BEF correspondence was delivered but all letters collected by the Postal lorries on their daily rounds were despatched to England in the usual way. Mail due to arrive with supplies were retained at the Base until such time as the Division came out of the line. This undoubtedly saved many bags from falling into the hands of Fritz

During the time the Division has been in the BEF no mails have been lost or fallen into enemy hands

No casualties.

Plateau Railhead — 15 m shell right in the office.
Men 100 yds away killed
Dr Berry. CAMS. 1 man wounded
Clothes in tatters
Mentioned in despatch Dec. 1917

Staff 25 (RE's)

Used Horses instead Rounds Carrying 16

6 more at Xmas
Post orderly.

Light Railways
Pack Horses.
Engine H. Truck at Xmas
to Quinena

Lost nothing through Enemy action

An anxious time with the
20th Division Posts.

During the latter part of Nov '17 the 20th Division Railhead Post Office, the main distributing point for mails between the divisional units, and the communications to the Base, and the United Kingdom, was situated in the remains of a Nissen Hut at an advanced railhead, named Revelon Farm, believed to be the most advanced railhead in the British line. *In front of Bde + Hqrs* It was situated near Heudicourt in the Cambrai sector.

The office had moved forward from Fins after the attack earlier in the month, which had necessitated the broad gauge railway being continued to enable an advanced railhead to be opened to facilitate the distribution of rations, and ammunition etc.

For

For a week everything was normal, not a sound of a gun, and no visits from German Aeroplanes, and in company with the Artillery Supply Section of 158 Coy A.S.C, we made merry on several evenings. On the morning of the 30th Nov we were very perturbed to know the meaning of the heavy gun fire heard during the night, and the conclusion arrived at was, our boys must be going over the top to continue the attack on Cambrai. We were also interested in seeing many aeroplanes performing wonderful feats in the air, and dropping all kinds of coloured lights, fortunately for us we did not know they were German planes at the time. About 8am the news spread around that the Germans had broken through our lines. This
information

information did not alarm us a great deal as we felt confident that any German advance would be short lived. However seeing later heavy artillery gunners coming past the office carrying gun sights, some without boots, others without puttees, tunics caps, and who stated they had been compelled to evacuate their guns, we thought it was time to try and get confirmation of what was going on. In the meantime the two Postal Lorries had ___ to the Divisional FPO's on the Fins road, in charge of ___ Supervisor. The congestion of ___ and M.T. transport making ___ Fins was continually growing ___ all told the tale, that the ___ were rapidly coming on, and their cavalry would be on us any
minute

minute. Things were looking serious, so it was decided to pack all registered articles, cash, valuables, and records, and send them away in charge of one of the staff, who was instructed to make for Fins, and failing our arrival to report to the D.A.D.P.S 3rd Corps. With the aid of a 3rd Corps Siege Park ration lorry this was accomplished. The R.T.O was then interviewed regarding the position, and he replied he was awaiting instructions from "Traffic" and would let us know later. Wounded men were now passing, and all ration dumps were being rapidly cleared, and the personel leaving with the lorries. Then a train of stone wagons pulled out with the R.T.O and his staff aboard.

We were now getting very concerned about the departure of the office fittings and the staff, and anxiously awaited the arrival of a Postal lorry, and much relieved on seeing the Divisional Supervisor return.

No 6. Post Orderly enters

Good morning much mail this morning?
The Old man cracked on at me shocking yesterday because I didn't take him a letter, and threatened to return me to duty if I didn't bring him a letter today.

assured there were letters alright today. ~~Then~~ Post Orderly ~~the~~ Quartermaster wants to know if he can have a morning Telegraph each day? Post Orderly glancing left & right passes a water bottle over the counter.

The Staff all being "teetotal" assume it must be some "Lime Juice" sent to warm up before going to bed.

The Quartermaster received his Telegraph regular.

One of the Supply Section enters

Good morning. Will this Green tin go today
Staff. Oh yes we'll see that through Tom.
& Would you like a Paper? Its freezing in here this morning. Tom Aint yes got no coal.?
The staff. Thats just our trouble. Bag of coal arrives
Later. A corporal enters
Staff. Finished railhead?
Cpl. Yes. Did very well this morning
Staff We had no milk in our tea this morning.
Cpl. I'll see what I can do
enters later with tin of milk.

return, but our spirits fell on him saying no lorries were allowed to come past Fins. Shells were now heard bursting not far away, which caused a few "Barnsfather" looks to each other.

Our hopes brightened on seeing an A.P.M. to whom we told our troubles.

He would not however give a pass for a Postal Lorry to come up, to clear the office, but told us, we had no right to be there, and to get away. This did not satisfy us, and a final visit to the railhead was made, and to our great joy, we found the Third Army Auxiliary Lorry Coy clearing their camp, and on appealing to the O.C. he kindly consented to allow us a little space on his badly needed lorries.

One arrived and we hastily placed the urgently needed articles, and all correspondence on, when three or four shells burst unpleasantly near. There was immediately a rush to get away, and after a final examination of the hut, we proceeded to Fins; and on arrival

arrival found Fins railhead evacuated owing to shelling, so proceeded to Nurlu and passed the night in the huts evacuated by 158 Coy ASC, and opened office at Rocquigny on the morning of the 1st Dec at which point the supply train was due to arrive. After the disposal of mails it was decided to try and get the remaining fittings, including our gramaphone, left at Revelon Farm.

This was accomplished after sunset, great difficulty being experienced in getting permission from the Traffic Controls at Fins, to be allowed to proceed along the Heudicourt Road, and then it was found Seige Guns were in action behind where our office had been, which necessitated getting permission to pass in front of the Guns. It was a most unpleasant time, and though everybody kept a brave face, the return journey through Fins was a welcome relief

www.ingramcontent.com/pod-product-compliance
Lightning Source LLC
Chambersburg PA
CBHW081356160426
43192CB00013B/2426